HERE I AM, SEND ME

Teaching from the book
of Isaiah and powerful stories
from The Message Trust

ANDY HAWTHORNE

BOOKS

Published by The Message Trust

First published in Great Britain 2014
Copyright © Andy Hawthorne, 2014

The moral right of the author has been asserted in accordance with the
Copyright, Designs and Patents Act 1988.

No part of this book may be used or reproduced in any manner whatsoever
without written permission from the publisher except in the case of brief
quotations embodied in similar works, critical articles or reviews.
Every reasonable effort has been made to credit copyright holders
of material reproduced in this book.

Except where marked, all Bible quotations are taken from the
New International Version, Copyright © 2011 by Biblica.
All rights reserved.

Publisher:
The Message Trust
Lancaster House
Lancaster Campus
Harper Road
Sharston
Manchester
M22 4RG
UK

www.message.org.uk

Print Edition ISBN: 978-0-9571414-7-6

Editor: Alistair Metcalfe

Proof Reading: Dev Lunsford

Reflection Questions: Ems Hancock

Designed In-House by Message Creative
Art Direction & Graphic Design: Dan Hasler
Additional Graphic Design & Photography: Hannah Prittie
www.messagecreative.com

Acknowledgements

Over the last couple of years as I led team devotions at The Message Trust on Isaiah, I've been influenced by lots of books, but in particular:

> The Prophecy of Isaiah – J A Motyer
> The Message of Isaiah – Barry Webb
> The Expositor's Bible Commentary – Frank E Gaebelein

Very special thanks to Alistair Metcalfe for spending so many hours and putting so much heart into this project.

To the amazing Message:Creative team for once again going above and beyond in your design work. To my long-suffering PA Emma Kizlauskas for making sense of my scribbles and of course, to all the faithful Message supporters who have stood with us in so many ways over the last 27 years – you know, and God knows, who you are!

Finally, to Michele, Sam and Beth. Thanks for not just watching your husband and dad do this stuff, but for catching the vision and running with it yourselves!

Contents

INTRODUCTION

Introduction

The movement now known as 'The Message Trust' started way back in 1987 when my brother and I had a vision for the biggest youth mission Manchester had ever seen. Our dream was to book the city's biggest rock venue for a week and fill it with the best bands, theatre companies and evangelists we could get our hands on. We decided to write to every church in Manchester to ask them to get behind it. In short, the afternoon we had that idea, I think we were convinced revival was on its way.

But by the time I'd got home from work that night, every ounce of faith had drained out of me. I realised that we were just two guys in our mid-twenties, with no connections and not a lot of money. There was no way on earth we could pull this vision off. We must have got it wrong! Sitting in my room, alone on my bed, despondently I picked up my Bible to read the set reading for the day, as I usually did. My prayer was simple: 'God, if this is you, please speak to me from your Word.' Here is what I read:

'Forget the former things;
    do not dwell on the past.
See, I am doing a new thing!
    Now it springs up; do you not perceive it?
I am making a way in the wilderness
    and streams in the wasteland.
The wild animals honour me,
    the jackals and the owls,
because I provide water in the wilderness
    and streams in the wasteland,
to give drink to my people, my chosen,
    the people I formed for myself
    that they may proclaim my praise.'

Isaiah 43:18-21

The moment The Message was born

You know what? We might have had the idea a few hours earlier, but I think *that* was the moment when the movement really got started – when we heard from God's Word that he was going to do this thing. I phoned Simon straight away and told him, 'God is going to do this!' We put those verses on the bottom of our first letterhead when we wrote to every church in Manchester. Today those words are the first thing you see when you enter our main meeting venue at our HQ, hanging down from the walls. In lots of ways, we've never left those promises, and we never will.

I love God. I love his Word. I love the way he keeps revealing new things in it, even from verses that we know well. And I'm so grateful God gave us these particular verses as our touchstone scriptures, because it's all in there – it's everything I want The Message to be and it's everything I want The Message to become.

Who are we?

We are a 'See! I am doing...' movement, a visionary people eagerly watching God for what he's doing and expectant for what he will accomplish next. God says to every believer, every day, 'See! I'm doing new things!' Every one of us needs to be seeing God at work in our lives and in our world. God is constantly calling us to lift up our eyes and see what he's doing. The authentic Christian life is about what he is doing through us, not what we are doing through him.

We are a 'new thing' movement, a pioneering, apostolic bunch of revolutionaries. There is something about doing innovative ministry that opens up a freedom and a space for others. When the World Wide Message Tribe came along, it seemed like 95% of Christian bands were all about getting in the charts, invading culture. Great! Some people need to do that. But when we came along, we weren't about having a hit single, we were about hitting souls for Jesus. We were about preaching the gospel. And we made a space for lots of other bands to do the same thing – making it OK to shout loud and long about Jesus. Similarly, Message 2000 was a new thing. Back then, not many evangelical Christians were getting involved in serving their communities through social engagement and random acts of kindness. But by doing it, and showing others the enormous value of getting our hands dirty on behalf of others, we helped to make it the 'new norm.' We've seen more churches getting involved in debt relief, food banks, schools and health centres. Today there is an expectation that the gospel changes lives and changes the communities they are part of. Clearly we can't take all the credit for this stuff, but I do believe we've played our part.

And we are a 'rivers in the desert' movement. We are a transformational people. We are about changing society. A river of life flows on the back of a people who are sold out for the gospel. These verses came alive to me in a new way recently when I watched a video a friend sent me. It was a clip of rainwater arriving in a dry valley in the Negev desert in Israel, the very desert that Isaiah prophesied about. People had gathered to see the moment when the rain arrived from the mountains and rushed into the valley, flooding everything in its path. When I saw it, my spirit jumped. I believe the life-giving water is going to flow when we see three things flowing down from the mountain of God. They are prayer, presence and proclamation.

Prayer

One of my key jobs as the leader of this organisation, this move of God, is to test the temperature of prayer and ensure we stay hot. I've come to realise that the most important thing is not how many people you have working for you, how many people come to your events, how big your budget is, or even how big your vision is. The most important thing is how important prayer is to you. I'm excited about the prayer temperature of The Message in this season. I want everyone to be on tiptoes in expectation – because things are hotting up. And we're beginning to see the evidence of that in the schools, in the prisons and on the estates. Which leads me to...

Presence

Prayer that doesn't lead to presence is just piety. Prayer always leads to people being the presence of Jesus in the places that need him most. Once you've prayed, you've touched the heart of God – and God's heart is for every broken, lost, forgotten person in your community. My experience and my heart is that Christians are not to be hermits, locked away in ivory towers – we are to be present with the poor, with the weak and with the lonely, just like Jesus was. Through Eden we've seen how presence means social transformation, as local areas are changed from the inside out. So prayer leads to presence, but presence must always lead to...

Proclamation

I often ask myself, where are the proclaiming evangelists today? Billy Graham is still preaching through the media to millions, more than anyone else alive probably. That can't be right – a 95-year-old bloke leading the charge! Where are the young men and women, passionately laying their lives down to preach the gospel to the lost? At The Message, we are committed to raising them up. Over the next season, on the back of all this prayer and presence we're going to shout louder than ever about the gospel. Starting in 2015, we're planning large-scale regional missions, partnering with churches and other organisations hopefully to put on the biggest youth missions the country has ever seen.

What happens next?

When we've got heartfelt prayer, heavenly presence and holy proclamation happening, we should confidently expect the rivers to flow. Those rivers bring new life to God's people, his chosen, those he has formed for his praise (v.21). And, as far as we're concerned, God wants everyone to be saved. So we are about loving everybody. We believe there is a gospel imperative to go to the poor and the most broken, to those on the margins – because it's the way Jesus did it.

We'll go out, and as we pray, as we presence ourselves and as we proclaim, we will see 'wild animals' begin to honour him. We're a transformational movement, seeing purposeless lives change, one at a time. We have learnt that when one life changes, the whole of society gets blessed.

The mess that becomes the message

I really hope and pray that as we journey through Isaiah together and that as you read stories of men and women whose lives were utterly chaotic before they met Jesus; people whose testimonies speak of addiction, violence, crime and ruinous behaviour, but who are now precious men and women of God; that your faith will rise and that you will see the new thing that God wants to do in and through you. What's more, I'd love it if every one of us would give our lives over to serving Jesus afresh, saying with Isaiah, 'Here I am, send me.'

Rivers in the desert bring renewal; they bring revival. If we see the prisons emptying and crime plummeting, the whole nation will be blessed. Great glory will go to Jesus. Our dream today is the same as it was in the beginning – to be a part of God's revival movement. And I pray this book will whet your appetite not just to watch it happen, but to be a part of it, too.

AS IT GOES WITH YOU...

CHAPTER ONE

The vision concerning Judah and Jerusalem that Isaiah son of Amoz saw during the reigns of Uzziah, Jotham, Ahaz and Hezekiah, kings of Judah.

Hear me, you heavens! Listen, earth!
    For the Lord has spoken:
'I reared children and brought them up,
    but they have rebelled against me.'

Isaiah 1:1-2

The shaking

We live in a fascinating time in our nation's life. It feels a bit like everything we have come to rely on, everything we have trusted in, is being shaken. Our newspapers and media haven't just reported scandal, but have been at the heart of it. Politicians and officials have been exposed as corrupt to the core. Bankers have proved unworthy of the trust we placed in them. Celebrities we used to love and admire have been found to be involved in shameful and disgusting acts. Can you feel the shaking going on? Perhaps we should not be surprised. When a nation turns away from God, this is what happens.

We did a song once with the World Wide Message Tribe, possibly one of our worst ever, *We Don't Get What We Deserve*. Well, sometimes in the life of a nation we *do* get what we deserve. We get the media that we deserve, we get the bankers that we deserve, we get the leaders we deserve and we get the celebrities that we deserve – because these are the people we celebrate in our society. If, as a nation, we stubbornly rebel and choose sin instead of righteousness, God will give us over to it.

Uncommon amounts of grace

Theologians talk about an idea painted in the Bible called the doctrine of common grace. In other words, God's grace is on everybody – not just his people, but on all people. God pours his grace out on everybody and I am so grateful for this! In fact, if it weren't for the restraining 'common grace' of God we'd all be stuffed! I'm pretty sure we would have destroyed ourselves centuries ago.

But there are times here on Earth when God, to some degree or other, removes his hand of grace. Romans 1:28 talks about people being 'given over' to their sinful desires. Psalm 81:11 too says people can be 'given over' to their stubborn hearts.

In other words, we start to get what we deserve, which is a frightening, frightening place to be. And this is not what God wants for us. It's not what God wanted for Israel in 670BC or what he wants for Great Britain (or anywhere else for that matter) as I am writing this in 2014. So, in his mercy, he challenges them – and us – not just about our lifestyles but also about our corrupt worship, because one always leads to another.

As it goes with the church so it goes with the nation. And that's where Isaiah comes in.

What is Isaiah all about?

Isaiah is a big book. It's not just the Bible's third biggest book in terms of length, but it's a book that is big in vision, and big in scope. If you want an overarching theme for the book it is this: 'Do not forsake God and it will go well with you and with the nation' or, more pithily, 'As it goes with God's people, so it goes with the nation.'

When the UK parliament debates and votes on the big issues of the day, they think that they are determining the future of our nation by the decisions they make. But they are not. Do you know who decides what the future of this and every nation is? Almighty God, and he works out that future through his church. As goes the church, so goes the nation – and that's a fearful thing to get our heads around. It means that many of the crazy and destructive things that happen in our nation and around the world are not actually the fault of fallen people or sinful, secular society. They are the fault of the church. They are *our* fault. We are the standard bearers who sometimes lose, or forget to hold any standard at all.

I don't want to sound like an old-fashioned-red-faced-angry-Bible-thumping preacher, but we need to realise how serious sin is. We need a renewed vision that it was our sin that sent Jesus to the cross. We need to understand that it is often our sin holding back God's purposes for this nation. God is not playing games here – he says these things for our benefit. If we break God's laws, we get hurt – and so do others.

Working with God

God has given us a partnership responsibility with him and the church needs to live it out and take our responsibilities seriously. We are not just meant to be doing random bits of mission here, there and everywhere – we are the Body of Christ and God's purposes are being worked out through us. And what are these purposes? The clue is in Isaiah's name, which means 'God saves'. This is the big vision – a divine revelation to a nation, not just to the church. And it's about salvation.

Three means of communication

God is speaking to us in Isaiah and as he speaks throughout the book, I see him speaking in three ways: in poetry, in prophecy and in prose.

In **poetry**, he wins our hearts with beautiful word pictures of who he is and what his plans are for Israel. We sing about the parched land rejoicing and the trees of the field clapping their hands. It's all there in Isaiah – he's a poet of the highest order. In **prophecy**, he speaks into the future of Israel but also the future of the whole world, anticipating the coming of the Messiah. He prophesies to two horizons. And in **prose**, he deals with the real events that were taking place in his own time. Isaiah is documenting real history, how God was working out his purposes amongst his people.

I reckon that's what we're meant to be like, too. This is how we need to take forward the vision God has given us for multiplication, for transformation. We're meant to be a people who are **poetic**: creative, innovative, ambitious, trying new things. We need to raise our game in music and the arts. The stamp of The Message movement is creativity. We're also meant to be people with a **prophetic** edge who are committed to bringing the Word of God alive today. And we're meant to be a people who are committed to writing **prose**: being willing to get our hands dirty, to work hard, to earth this thing, and write history. We're to employ all our gifts, carrying them out into the wasteland places.

One thing you can't get away from as you read through Isaiah is that this is one of the most passionate books in the Bible. He's passionate for his people, Israel, and he's passionate to speak of the future Messiah. But if there's one thing that comes over more than anything in the book of Isaiah, he is a man who is passionate for holiness. And that's the theme of our next chapter.

REFLECTION

1. How do you respond to the concept that the health of the church reflects the health of our society? Has it challenged you? In what way?

2. Have you ever had an experience that made you feel that God was allowing you to experience grace, in spite of what you had done? What was the result of that situation? What did you learn from that?

3. How ambitious are you in how you share the gospel with others? Do you think God might be challenging you to develop more creativity? In what areas? Write down some of your reflections and pray into them.

1. It challenges me to ask, "Where is the church simply following the cultural pressures to 'do what feels good' or join the commercial bandwagon & where should it make a stand & not compromise biblical standards?"

2. Yes — and it made me learn that God is very good & loving & forgiving.

3. Not that ambitious — mainly through Alpha. I love Andrea's creativity. I wish I had more creativity, especially for the "Family Time."

PRAYER

Father,
thank you for your crazy, wonderful grace
that is sufficient for me in every day
and in every season.
Thank you that you made me to be
a transformational person in community with others.
Please use me to help rewrite the history
of individuals in this nation by my attitudes,
prayers, thoughts and the standards
I set in my heart and my home.

Amen

'We couldn't sit there and want it
to happen, and not be prepared
to do it ourselves'

Ben and Beth Baker head up Eden Fir Vale, based a few miles from the centre of Sheffield. Fir Vale is a richly multicultural area with white British, Asian and Eastern European communities living side by side, but it is one of the most economically deprived areas in the country. Ben and Beth obediently said 'here we are, send us!' back in 2011. Here's some of their story.

I guess it all started when we decided to say 'yes.' We'd heard lots about Eden and how it would take a team of people to move into Fir Vale in order for it to happen. I (Ben) remember sitting in the church at St Thomas Crookes, hearing someone talking about Eden thinking, 'Yes, I'd love to see that happen – someone should do it!' without necessarily thinking it should be us. But during the following year, lots of little things kept prompting us and eventually it became a matter of integrity – we couldn't sit there and want it to happen, and not be prepared to do it ourselves!

So we moved to Fir Vale in September 2011. Getting Eden off the ground was a matter of being proactive, listening and learning. We started off doing detached work and prayer walking around the neighbourhood, getting our faces recognised around the local area. Another of the first things we did and which continues to this day, is offering lesson support in the local secondary school. It was simply a case of explaining to the school who we were and offering to help. So I started going in as a voluntary teaching assistant, working particularly with bottom set Year 10s and just being on hand in the classroom. We also get involved with the annual 'Make Your City Shine' schools week that brings Message bands and others into five schools across Sheffield for a week and reaches thousands with the good news of Jesus.

We were soon joined by our first Eden volunteer, Andy. He'd been interested in Eden for longer than we had, but he was in the middle of a nursing course. When he finished, he didn't know what he should do – wait for a job to come up, or just move in. In the end, he decided he would move in and shortly after, God provided him with the perfect job at the Northern General – bang in the middle of Fir Vale! He took the step of faith, God provided the job.

Since then, we've been joined by Gareth and Rachel, Nick and Lauren, Jon, Becky and Nikky, and our daughter Evie was born shortly after our second anniversary on Eden Fir Vale, so that made eleven! We've become really close in a short space of time, I think because we've all made the same commitment, and we've all made sacrifices to be here. Having people with different passions join the team is really helpful – I don't think any of us are 'typical' youth-workers but each of us is committed to what we are doing and have a very clear focus of what we are about and why we are here.

In everything we do, our main aim is to be relational, rather than attractional. But when we do events, whether that's Friday night football or a community meal, we always want to do them well because they are a good springboard to on-going stuff where relationships can deepen. We think of all our activities in the shape of a funnel – wide and shallow at the top, but becoming deeper and narrower all the time. Last spring

FLOW

the message

THE MAGAZINE OF **THE MESSAGE** | ISSUE 12 **SUMMER** 2013

PLANTING EDEN

STARTING FROM SCRATCH IN SHEFFIELD

ALSO IN THIS ISSUE:
NEW SCHOOLS TEAMS | MESSAGE MIDLANDS
IN YER FACE'S NEW SHOW   STUART BELL

SPECIAL REPORT INSIDE

we opened a new after-school drop-in for local young people up to the age of 17 with all the classic features of a youth drop-in – games, Wii, hot chocolate – but with a focus on relationships. As this began to prove most popular with primary age children, we evolved the drop-in into a new after school group just for them. 'Shout' now takes place every Wednesday afternoon with a high-energy, front-led mix of games, Bible stories and more. It has actually become our biggest place of engagement with children all week. It's also very intentional about teaching children about Jesus and encouraging them to engage personally, with a weekly challenge for them to take away and do. It's about deep living, rather than deep teaching. It's amazing how the stories stick in the kids' minds and then come up in conversation in the park or playing football.

Another regular group which is seeing real fruit is our 'Flourish' girls group, gathered weekly around a craft activity. It's become a place of belonging and deep relationships with teenage girls. A group like Flourish will gather much smaller numbers, but I think it yields deeper relationships with a longer-term perspective. We're really excited about it because I think future leaders are likely to come from this intentional investment in a few.

We've also developed a six-week leadership course for use in our local secondary school, based on the 'life shapes' curriculum from St Thomas'. Each of the six steps has a Bible verse that relates to it and brings in a theme about God. Through it, we're teaching the young people to identify something about their community they'd like to change for the better – and then giving them a process to implement it.

And excitingly, we've seen the emergence of a new missional community known as 'Restore'. A number of our cell groups that were already meeting in homes and doing life together began gathering monthly for worship on a Sunday. We do simple teaching for adults and kids and a huge community lunch open to everyone. It's chaotic, but it works – people seem willing and able to access it wherever they are at, and kids in our community especially seem to understand it instinctively. Off the back of this, we recently launched three Alpha groups in different homes on Tuesday evenings and Sunday teatime with a goal to connect with people in a new way and to talk about the good news of Jesus over a good meal together. Through this, we're starting to see a ripple effect as our neighbours have started inviting friends of their own. Even before our neighbours have found a living faith themselves, they're inviting others to come and discover Jesus too!

Since we arrived nearly three years ago we've learnt so many things. Looking around an area like ours, you see so many things you'd like to change. That can send you into despair. A lot of the time you can't always see why you are doing what you do. There are breakthroughs and they need to be celebrated but there are also a lot of times when you just need to press on. But as a missional community, we remind each other that we moved here because of what God can see, and that always encourages us to keep going.

THE
SCARIEST
THING
IN THE
WORLD

CHAPTER TWO

ISAIAH 1:3-4

'The ox knows its master,
  the donkey its owner's manger,
but Israel does not know,
  my people do not understand.'
Woe to the sinful nation,
  a people whose guilt is great,
a brood of evildoers,
  children given to corruption!
They have forsaken the Lord;
  they have spurned the Holy One of Israel
  and turned their backs on him.

Isaiah 1:3-4

Parenting the prodigal

Ask anyone who has kids and they'll tell you that bringing them up is the most heart-wrenching, frustrating, mind-bending, exciting, and joyful experience anyone could have. It takes you to the very end of yourself. It turns your world upside down. Sometimes, kids don't know what's good for them, literally. It's the same with us and God. He gives us his best, and wants us to walk in all of it – all the benefits, all the righteousness and joy in the Holy Spirit, all the provision, all the health and prosperity for our souls. So he tells us how to live, his way: 'His house, his rules.' We, of course, so often ignore him.

Isaiah makes it very clear that there are effects of our sinfulness and our rebellion. Our habits and priorities, the lifestyle that we build results in our destinies.

Look what the Lord says: 'The ox knows his master, the donkey his owner's manger but Israel does not know, my people do not understand' (v3). The ox and the donkey know where their shelter is. They will come home every night to keep warm and safe. They know what food they should have to keep them healthy.

It is as if we can hear God saying here: 'Come on guys! If the dull-witted ox and donkey can get this, what is the matter with you? Why would you wander away from my shelter, my place of safety? Why would you not feed on food that's good? Why would you head towards things that will destroy you? It will lead to desolation for you and for the nation!' I don't think we realise how high God's calling for his church is. We are alive to populate that new heaven and that new earth to come, to bring his holy presence down and to be those glory carriers who take his power right to the heart of a world in desperate need. What a wonderful calling that is! But how are we doing at it?

The might-have-beens

What do Audley Harrison, George Best and Samson have in common? Here are three great men who, at one time in their lives, had the world at their feet. But, they threw it all away. Back in the late nineties, Harrison was the best amateur boxer in the world, going on to become the first British fighter ever to win a super-heavyweight gold medal at the 2000 Olympics. He looked set to conquer the world.

But he let it all go to his head. He probably didn't put the work in behind the scenes. In his final fight against David Haye in 2010, he only threw one punch and crumbled within three rounds.

If you're into football, you'll certainly know about George Best. I remember seeing an interview with him on television where he was asked, 'George, do you realise you could have been one of the greatest footballers this planet has ever seen?' Arrogantly he replied, 'I WAS the greatest footballer this planet has ever seen!' Sadly, I think he was mistaken. I saw him at what should have been the height of his powers, at 27 years old. He'd left Manchester United in disgrace and was now playing for Stockport County, overweight and shuffling round the pitch. Whilst he had huge potential, his addiction to alcohol meant that there is no way this man was ever going to be the best of the best.

Both men remind me of Samson in the Bible. Samson was a handsome man with incredible gifts. He had supernatural strength, God's hand was on his life. He had a great destiny and a purpose. But he couldn't control his lusts or his temper. He ended up blind and just grinding corn – round and round and round. Strong like Audley Harrison, handsome and gifted like George Best, but like them, all we can find to say about Samson is, 'what a waste!'

Unfulfilled potential

One of the scariest things in the world to me is the idea of unfulfilled potential. The thought that I could get to be an old man and find myself thinking, 'I've missed it, I've blown it! I haven't achieved what God wanted me to achieve!' makes me shudder. In our work at The Message, we get to see the tragic reality of unfulfilled potential close up.

Thank God, we see dozens of young men and women every year, coming through as students in our Message Academy or apprentices in our Enterprise Centre – young people whose lives used to be train wrecks but which God has miraculously turned around. They are beautiful demonstrations of all that God can do with a man or a woman who surrenders to him – lives that are step by step, moving from chaos to health, productivity and joy.

But sadly, we also see some who go the way of Audley and George and Samson. There are some each year who make bad choices, go back to their old ways and miss the amazing opportunities that Jesus puts at their feet.

It is tough watching those we love and invest ourselves in, throw away their opportunities. That's why we so need to hear what the book of Isaiah has got to say to us as a people of God today.

God's calling throughout the book of Isaiah is for his people to be holy and set apart because *he* is holy. If we want to enjoy life to the full, the power and the freedom and the joy of walking in relationship with God, we need to go after holiness. And he wants this for us because out of the purity and power of that relationship, he wants to bless the whole world.

Recently I felt God speaking to me very clearly about our teams at The Message and what we need if we're going to go to the next level of multiplication in creative arts mission teams, community transformation and Christ-centred enterprise. I felt him say that the most important thing that we bring is not better bands or theatre companies, or even more prayer initiatives or new enterprises or Eden teams. The most important thing we can bring to him is our holiness, our set-apartness.

The high calling of holiness

The most vital thing we bring to our mission – the best thing we can give to those God has sent us to – is our holiness. We literally cannot afford to be unholy at a time like this. This isn't a message saying 'Don't drink!' 'Don't go out dancing!' 'Don't go to the SIN-ema!' That's not holiness. We're talking about being *in* the world, but not *of* the world; being set apart for Jesus and radically loving his people. How could we carry on sinning knowing that is what is at stake?

Isaiah is devastated by the state of his nation because of the effects of sin. We need to be, too.

Ultimately of course, any holiness we have is a gift. We cannot be holy before the Lord on our own. I can never be holy enough or good enough to come into God's presence, and nor can you – it is a gift from Jesus that we must receive. But there is a sanctification process that God is fully expecting us to be involved in, bit by bit, day by day. I believe we are a revival movement because we have revival promises spoken over us. But every revival that ever shook this nation – whether it was the Welsh revival, or the Salvation Army, or the Methodists – had holiness at the heart. They all had holiness groups and were accountable to one another for their lifestyle.

The wholeness of holiness

But holiness is also a gift for our own good. It's the very best way to live. God knows what he's talking about. He made the universe, he designed it, he knows what makes it work. He is uniquely qualified to write the instruction manual to a good life. And he longs for relationship with us. He is the holy, awesome, fearful, Almighty God. He's the creator, who spoke and the universe was formed. But he is also our Dad.

When I come to my heavenly Dad, I know he is so *for* me! He wants me to thrive and be healthy, productive and successful. He wants me to be an old man with no regrets. He wants me to go to the grave with all the good works he has got planned in advance for me, *done in full.*

And that makes me *want* to give holiness back to God. I don't want to break the heart of my Father in heaven. I want to please him. So, in my decisions, I'm working out every day – what does holiness look like? I know it is not a weird cult-like religion but a radical passionate beautiful faith. What does it look like in this generation to be marked by holiness?

REFLECTION

1. Can you think of a time in your past when you tried to 'go it alone' and live without the rule and reign of God? What were you like? What impact did the way you lived have on those around you?

2. Isaiah challenges us to be a people of holiness. Try and write down what that means to you in one sentence. Then put that somewhere you will see it and read it every day. What aspects of your life now do you feel need the gift of holiness over them? Ask God to help you give those areas of yourself over to him.

3. We are all people of potential. What do you feel might be holding you back from reaching your destiny? Perhaps you could find someone you can be accountable to on a regular basis – to pray with you and support you on your journey.

1. Yes. From 14-40 I lived without the rule & reign of God. Before I met Kirstie I was a pleasure-seeking, me-first, take what I can get, person who fell a long way short of my potential.

2. Holiness means taking our lead from God, through Jesus Christ. It means obeying him as the no. 1 priority.
   - My prayer life.
   - My thought life.
   - My temptation to drink regularly.

3. Not thinking big enough. Not having enough courage. Being lazy (reluctant to change myself). Refusing to find time for quiet days or a spiritual director or a prayer partner.

PRAYER

Father God, thank you for your awesome gift of holiness.
Thank you that I can never measure up to that without Jesus
and the Holy Spirit making himself at home in me.
God, I don't want to miss my chance to serve you
because of my weakness in any area.
Please show me places in my life that need your holiness
and wholeness and help me to reach every potential
and goal you set for me in Christ, for the sake of myself,
my family, my church and the nations.

Amen

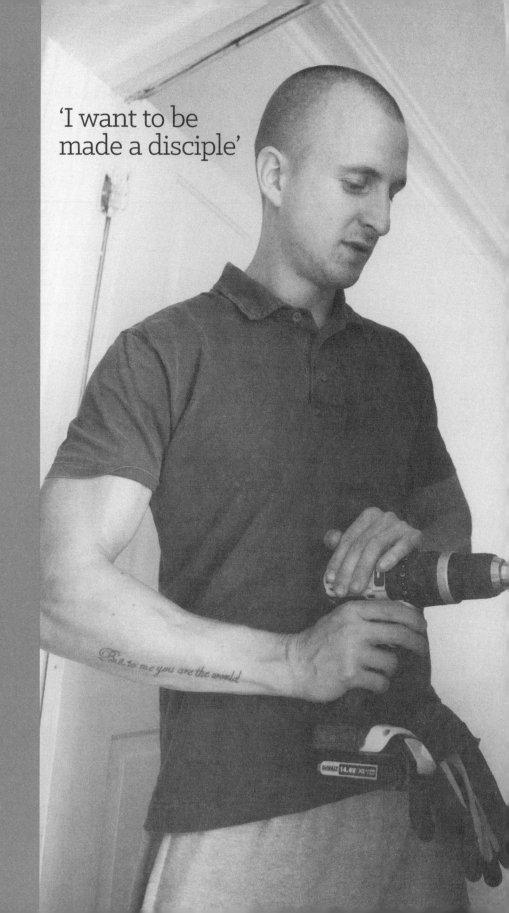

TESTIMONY
JASON HOOPER

'I want to be
made a disciple'

Jason was our very first MEC Apprentice, starting work with our Building Services team even before the Centre officially opened in January 2013. Before he came to us, he hadn't worked more than two weeks in his life. He is a man totally transformed by the power and goodness of God.

From as young as I can remember, I was never able to handle my temper. I was always in trouble in school, always smashing up my mum's house, always running away from home. I even stabbed my own sister. My mum couldn't handle me and put me in care because she didn't know what else to do. I was basically out of control.

In care, I had no good influences and I soon got into drink and drugs. I got more violent and started messing about with crime, stealing cars and stupid stuff like that. Looking back, I know I didn't want to be that way. I was always very confused. I remember thinking, 'This isn't me.' Deep inside my heart, I was always upset, always crying on my own. But I didn't know how to get out of it.

I got given my first prison sentence when I was 15 and I went in and out the 'revolving door' many times over the next 12 years. It never did me any good. I could easily carry on taking and dealing drugs inside. It never dealt with my anger or my emotions. When I was on the outside, I would get into trouble with the police for growing cannabis and causing trouble. My relationships would always go wrong.

The bottom line is, I believe Satan had a hold on my mind – he made me think things I didn't want to think and kept me locked in a cycle of self-destruction. I was on a mission to kill myself. I stopped eating for weeks at a time. I cut my wrists. I took overdoses. I whipped myself with a belt and buckle, cutting myself open. There was a point I was screaming so loud and for so long that blood was coming out of my lungs.

Eventually I voluntarily handed myself in to a psychiatric unit and I was put in a cell. I paced around all night like a wild animal, my blood boiling, pain all through my body. I was shaking, thinking that if I stopped moving, I would die. The staff had absolutely no idea what to do with me.

That was when it happened. It was about midnight. Everything just stopped. All the pain, all the bad thoughts disappeared. I felt like my brain was empty and ready for what God would show me. I asked someone to please go and bring me a Bible I had seen once on the hospital wing. They brought it to me and it fell open at 2 Corinthians 7 where Paul writes, '…godly grief produces a repentance that leads to salvation without regret, whereas worldly grief produces death.'

I started reading about sorrow, repentance and salvation. It was for me! I didn't know anything about Christianity or God but I knew Jesus was speaking to me. I felt like I was getting cleansed and cleaned by him right there in my cell. I started crying my eyes out, giving it all to God. He instantly took all of my addictions away, and healed me of a heart problem I had from taking steroids. My life got turned around.

The staff saw the change in me immediately because I was suddenly happier, I had a joy about me. Over a small space of time, God built me back up. Before I knew it, I was finding out I can sing and play the guitar, that I wanted to write poetry! I couldn't stop telling people about God. Soon someone told me about the courses Reflex were running on the wings and the staff gave me permission to join a group. There I met Simon, Matty and Nick from The Message's Reflex team – all of whom became like brothers to me. They began to mentor me in my walk with God and when it came to getting out, they set me up with a church. I became a different person.

I was proud to be accepted as the first apprentice to be taken on by the Message Enterprise Centre in the summer of 2012. I started training and working in the building business, restoring properties. I've been part of that team nearly two years now. The last two years has been a period of growth and growing up – learning about business, learning how to conduct myself, and learning about me. I'll be honest, it's not always been easy. It's hard for someone who is so used to doing whatever they like to submit to authority sometimes. But for me this is part of growing up.

I can get very impatient and want things to happen fast. But sometimes God makes us wait. For instance I'm growing food in my garden – and I want to see fruit. Sometimes all I can see is green shoots and no fruit and I need to learn to wait. It's been about learning to walk in step with the Spirit. When you've been through what I've through I can be emotionally very up and down. I can still get wound up and I need to make sure I don't give the devil a foothold. The Spirit of God brings me peace and brings order.

I want to be made a disciple – I'm really serious about that. That's what Jesus wants for me and that's what I want. I want the discipline. That's what lads like me need. Teaching on identity, constantly reminding of the gospel. You want to say 'brainwash', yes! As J. John said once, our brains need washing, because they're filthy!

I still have to contend with temptation – it's a war, actually. I'm learning to 'not merely listen to the word, but put it into practice' and how to 'take every thought captive.' I've made mistakes, but over that period of time, thanks to the support of the people at The Message and thanks to the power of God in me, my mindset has changed.

But it's also been a time where has God used me powerfully. I don't stop talking to people about God. It doesn't stop when I 'clock off.' My life is about Jesus now. My life is consumed with Christ. Sometimes I get a bit frustrated that it's not me going into schools and into prisons to tell people about Jesus. But even on the building team, I'm making it my business to tell as many people about Jesus as I can. I could look back on my life and say, 'what a waste.' And it was. I hate the devil and what he did to me. It was a meaningless, dark existence. Destruction for everyone around me. And yet it wasn't a waste, because here I am now. I'm so happy. I don't need any of that stuff any more. I'm so grateful. Because I've come out of that, I'm praying, 'Use me. Use me to show them you.' I see God using me. I see myself travelling to different places, talking about my story, talking about God's goodness. I'm a vessel to be used, I want God to touch people through my life.

BE VERY CAREFUL HOW YOU WORSHIP

CHAPTER THREE

'The multitude of your sacrifices –
    what are they to me?' says the Lord.
'I have more than enough of burnt offerings,
    of rams and the fat of fattened animals;
I have no pleasure
    in the blood of bulls and lambs and goats.
When you come to appear before me,
    who has asked this of you,
    this trampling of my courts?
Stop bringing meaningless offerings!
    Your incense is detestable to me.
New Moons, Sabbaths and convocations –
    I cannot bear your worthless assemblies.
Your New Moon feasts and your appointed festivals
    I hate with all my being.
They have become a burden to me;
    I am weary of bearing them.
When you spread out your hands in prayer,
    I hide my eyes from you;
even when you offer many prayers,
    I am not listening.
Your hands are full of blood!
Wash and make yourselves clean.
    Take your evil deeds out of my sight;
    stop doing wrong.
Learn to do right; seek justice.
    Defend the oppressed.
Take up the cause of the fatherless;
    plead the case of the widow.'

Isaiah 1:11-17

What drives us?

As we saw in the first chapter, as it goes with the church so it goes with the nation. We have to realise how serious it is that we live lives that please God in every area. Of course, this is not mainly a question of things we do when we meet together. It is also about who we are when the doors are shut and there is no one else listening. It is about making sure we are positioned where we are meant to be, that we are being effective in holding back the tide and pushing forward the Kingdom.

But having said all of that, Isaiah shows us that there is something important about the way we worship. You see if we're not careful, this holy thing we call worship can easily become an aping of the culture. The key drivers of our society are easy to see: self-centredness, consumerism and celebrity obsession. If we're not careful those characteristics can leak into our worship when we gather as God's people.

It can become a very self-centred thing. Is there anything more blasphemous than walking out at the end of a Sunday morning service and saying 'I didn't get much out of the worship today!' But I bet you've said it – I have, too. When it's not about us. It's about him.

How about consumerism? You can see it as people flit from church to church because one place doesn't give them what they want or what they think they need, or the leader says something that upsets them, or they don't get on with that person or that pastor.

And of course, we're far from immune from celebrity culture. Who's the hottest celebrity worship leader or preacher these days? What festival, event or conference do we need to travel to, just to see them? Can't you see that this is just mimicking what we see in the world?

Nothing new under the sun

You might be surprised to hear that these things are not new. This is what was going on in Isaiah's day, too. Chapter 1:11 says the people were really going for it – there were a multitude of bulls, lambs and goats being sacrificed. It implies that they are giving way beyond the requirements of the law, there is a lavishness going on in their gatherings. And yet, the Lord says, Stop! 'Stop bringing me meaningless offerings!' (v.13)

They're hosting extravagant festivals and feasts, new moon sabbaths and convocations, the lot. In our terms, they're spending the whole summer travelling from festival to festival having a great time, thinking that they are praising the Lord. But he calls it all 'a burden'; he even says 'I hate them.' This is strong language! And it is not just a theme of Isaiah chapter 1, it comes up again and again and again in the Bible.

It sounds harsh but the reason is, he knows they are harbouring sin (v.16). And in light of this, all their offerings are meaningless.

A new kind of worship leader

There's not much talk of the worship leader in the Bible, you know. These days it seems every church worth its salt has a worship director or a worship leader; the so-called 'best' ones sell truckloads of records and people flock to hear them lead worship.

Now, don't get me wrong – I do believe in 'lead worshippers' and I think they are a great gift to us from God – the gift of music and the calling to lead people in songs. But we need a new kind of worship leader in church – and not the kind who stands at the front of meeting with a guitar. My sense, actually, is that the Body of Christ needs five different types of worship leader, following the fivefold ministry Paul describes in Ephesians 4: those who are called to be pastors, evangelists, teachers, prophets or apostles. In this way, I think we are all called to be worship leaders. What do I mean?

We need **pastoral** worship leaders. We need people who come alongside others with sensitivity and long for their development. Those who choose, even through the rollercoaster of discipleship and all the wacky things people can do, to stick with them and present them to Jesus.

We need **evangelistic** worship leaders – and maybe that's what most of us at The Message are. We're called to go where others won't go, to bring the lost in. That is at the heart of our worship as a movement. As we go out there to the prisons, the tough estates and rough and forgotten schools, we take the presence of God with us. We are called to be light in the darkness to sing to those who are broken and to bring them hope and healing through the truth of the words we bring.

We need **teaching** worship leaders who, with God's help, understand the 'why' behind the 'what'. They long for Christians not to be airheads but to understand why God is doing what he is doing. Teaching in this way presents the living book of the Bible to people in the power of the Spirit. When we do that correctly, those we teach grasp its transforming message for themselves and find that they are never the same again.

We need **prophetic** worship leaders who speak God's word to his people, who hear God clearly for his own. Maybe this is the type closest to the worship leaders or lead worshippers who help us to draw near to God week by week in sung worship and in our prayer times together as a team.

And we need **apostolic** worship leaders – people who break new ground so that others can fully enter into their calling. People who are willing to pioneer new ministries and go where others have not gone; people who think outside the norms and the expectations of the day. I think that's an area where, at our best, The Message can play a part, too.

If we could embrace this broader type of worship leading, I'm sure we wouldn't be hearing the awful words that Isaiah and his people were hearing. So what are we doing? What kind of offering are we bringing to God? Is it acceptable to him?

REFLECTION

1. What kind of Christian are you when people are looking? Are you more generous, calmer, kinder, more friendly or, at times, if you are honest, just a little bit fake? Isaiah is challenging us to check why we offer what we do to God. What does this make you think of in your own life?

2. Have you been guilty of any kind of self-centredness, consumerism or an unhealthy approach towards famous Christians in your journey with God? What do you sense God telling you about that today? What will your response to him be?

3. How do you feel about being a 'worship leader' in your own life? What kind of gifting do you feel you have alongside that? A pastor, evangelist, teacher, prophet or apostle? What can you do this week to fan that gift into flame and grow in that area?

1. Trying to look sorted. Trying to give people what is attractive. The 'mask'.

2. I do tend to focus on just a few 'famous' Christians. C.S. Lewis, Tom Wright, Nicky Gumble. I need to place Jesus at the centre, not Celebrities.

3. Evangelist. Plan how to take the post-Alpha group forward.

PRAYER
A PRAYER FOR WORSHIP LEADERS

Lord, I pray you'll help us by your Spirit
to understand how to be true worship leaders.
I pray pastoral, evangelistic, teaching, prophetic
and apostolic worship leaders will be raised up
in our land and, as a result, your people
will be blessed and this nation will be blessed.
God, help us to find out who we are,
and why we are here for your glory.

Amen

TESTIMONY
DAVE MOORE

'I always knew
that this was what
I was born to do'

Dave is one half of Vital Signs, our edgy hip-hop mission team. Everywhere they play they are seeing responses to Jesus among the hardest-to-reach young people in schools, prisons and tough communities.

I believe that if we're going to see revival breaking out in this land, we're going to see it happening first among the lost causes and the hopeless cases. And the reason I believe we are going to see full-blown revival breaking out is because it is happening already. I know, because for a long time I was a lost cause and a hopeless case myself.

I grew up in a broken family because my mum and dad split up when I was 5. All the way through school I acted the joker and was never far away from trouble of some sort. I got introduced to drugs when I was just 12 – I started with weed, then I got deeper and deeper into it. The joker in me became more violent and more aggressive. It turned really nasty when I was 14 and I was kicked out of home and put in foster care.

There was a brief period when it looked like things might be different. My mum became a Christian when I was 15 and she tried to give me a fresh start by taking me to Canada for three months to stay with my aunt who was also a Christian. She took me to a Christian camp where I heard someone talking about my granddad, who was a missionary in Africa, an amazing man of God. But I didn't want to know. It wasn't getting through. I came back to England and moved in with a mate whose mum was a drug dealer. Suddenly everyone in my world was doing drugs, so of course I started selling it myself. First it was just weed, but then it moved to coke and ecstasy.

Over a period of about three years, my life just spiralled out of control. I was addicted to drugs and I was in too deep to get out. When the deal didn't come off or I lost money, I robbed houses. I had a restraining order put on me. I was stabbed three times. Everything I touched went bad. My friends were the local scumbags. I was a scumbag.

Music always had a power over me. I loved hip-hop and it made me want to be like the gangsters. It's no secret that some of the music glamourises violence and crime, and it put these ideas into my head too. The only reason I wasn't a bigger drug dealer was because I lived in a small town and I didn't have the access to guns and the shadier side of things.

It was a song that God used to finally get through to me. To be honest, I couldn't even tell you what song it was. I was 20 years old, walking through the Co-op and I heard a song that said 'Heaven' in the chorus. I can't explain exactly what happened in that moment, but God just got me. I knew I was going to hell if I died, I wasn't going to heaven. I started weeping. Everything that my mum had tried to tell me for five years came flooding back into my memory: about Jesus dying on the cross for me, about new life in him. It was a decisive moment – I knew it was now or never. I had to change. I went into a Christian rehab.

After I became a Christian, my first thought was to leave music behind because it had been such a big part of my past. But God kept prompting me through other people to

keep going with it. I felt like I just had to be willing to be sent. I had tried to write music before, but it had never made sense. When I became a Christian, everything clicked – I wrote a song and it made sense. I started performing as D-Cype, starting with little outreaches, getting a little bit better. I had the chance to play gigs around Europe, and I even opened for Lecrae when he came to Manchester.

Everything went to the next level when I got accepted onto Message Academy and I got trained up as an evangelist. I think I always knew that this was what I was born to do. At the end of the year I was invited to form a new band with Nick Shahlavi who I met while I was at Message Academy. We started recording and performing together. At our first prison gig at the end of 2013, we got a taste of what was to come. About 50 guys showed up and we did a couple of songs and gave our testimonies. Out of the whole room, only five didn't make a response to God. That fired us up!

Since then, everywhere we've been we're seeing responses to the gospel. Recently we were booked to spend a week in Buttershaw, Bradford, helping the Eden team as they went into the local school. God was at work big time. We were only meant to do a few lessons on 'Choice and Consequences' but as word spread, they doubled and tripled up the classes so that eventually we got in front of every single student. We were able to be totally open about our testimonies and the decisions we made to follow Jesus. At the end of the week show, over 150 kids turned up – and when it came to the gospel presentation, around 100 came forward to be prayed for. I knew some were just there

for the hype, so I laid it down bluntly: 'Guys, if you are not here because you want to give your life to Jesus, please leave. We'll come out and hang with you in a few minutes, but this is a very important moment for those who are really serious about this.' A few left, but most stayed and wanted to pray with us to accept Jesus.

Our vision is to get in front of as many people as we can and preach the gospel. The music's important to us but it's mainly a way of attracting a crowd and getting in front of people. It's the gospel where the real power is, the message of Christ and him crucified. It's humbling to see how God can use stories from our lives to bring change to other people. That's what revival's about!

THE MOUNTAIN OF THE LORD

CHAPTER FOUR

This is what Isaiah son of Amoz saw
concerning Judah and Jerusalem:

In the last days
the mountain of the Lord's temple will be established
    as the highest of the mountains;
it will be exalted above the hills,
    and all nations will stream to it.
Many peoples will come and say,
'Come, let us go up to the mountain of the Lord,
    to the temple of the God of Jacob.
He will teach us his ways,
    so that we may walk in his paths.'
The law will go out from Zion,
    the word of the Lord from Jerusalem.
He will judge between the nations
    and will settle disputes for many peoples.
They will beat their swords into ploughshares
    and their spears into pruning hooks.
Nation will not take up sword against nation,
    nor will they train for war any more.
Come, descendants of Jacob,
    let us walk in the light of the Lord.

Isaiah 2:1-5

Standing on the front foot

I t's not hard to feel 'on the back foot' as a Christian. Especially with the militant atheist lobby who seem to pop their heads up whenever any of us try to celebrate our Christian heritage, or point out that the Christian faith really is at the heart of pretty much everything that's good about our society. Recently the British Prime Minister got in hot water with a bunch of humanists for daring to state that Britain is still a Christian country and for celebrating some of the fantastic things the church is doing up and down the land.

I for one am mighty glad that David Cameron wanted to say that, because he is dead right – and I'm convinced we move away from our Christian heritage at our peril. Perhaps like me, David Cameron has noticed that there aren't too many humanist homeless shelters, food banks, prison workers or debt counsellors out there.

The truth, of course, is that we have no need to feel 'on the back foot.' Why? Well, firstly, the gospel has lost none of its power and as such works like nothing else to change individuals' lives and indeed whole communities if we will let it. And secondly, the church isn't in retreat – it is actually advancing on pretty much all fronts! Wherever I go, I love saying this: 'Today is an exciting day in the history of the church, in fact perhaps the most exciting day, because almost certainly more people will come to Christ today than at any time since he rose from the dead. All over the world, the Spirit really is moving.'

This is the key theme of the first few verses of Isaiah chapter 2, written 600-plus years before Jesus walked the earth. Verse 2 says, 'In the last days the mountain of the Lord's temple will be established as the highest of the mountains; it will be exalted above the hills, and all nations will stream to it.'

Coming so we can go

Mountains played an important part in the false religions of the nations around Israel. Their altars and temples tended to be in the so-called High Places. The Greek god Zeus was believed to live on Mount Olympus in Greece, and the god Baal lived on Mount Cassus in Syria. This is why, when we see a reference in the Bible to the High Places being removed, it is a sign of the nation turning back to God. According to Isaiah, though, there is only one mountain that counts – the Mountain of the Lord. There is definitely an exclusiveness to our faith, one Mountain and one Saviour; but also an inclusiveness, because he points out that all nations can and will stream to it. There's only one path but it's a path that everyone can tread if they choose to.

There is only one true gospel but it is totally relevant to every single human being. Recently I had a bizarre couple of weeks when I went straight from visiting some of the projects The Message supports amongst the poorest of the poor in Haiti, to spending a few days in the swanky French ski chalet of a multi-millionaire couple who support our work. The amazing thing is that the gospel is just as relevant in both places. It really is for all people and, as verse 3 points out, for many people.

Verse 3 is actually very interesting because it's as if Isaiah is catching on to the New Testament theme of outreach to every nation. Most Jews in Isaiah's day would consider engaging with God was all about coming to the mountain, and the verse does say 'Come, let us go up to the mountain of the Lord, to the temple of the God of Jacob,' but it also says, 'the law will go out from Zion, the word of the Lord from Jerusalem.' In other words we are only coming so we can *go*. Every time we gather and come to the Lord, the clock is ticking, because we are meant to be going pretty soon.

If only more Christian believers realised that's what it is all about, first and foremost! In verse 4 there is a lovely picture of just what can happen when we do go out in the Lord's name:

'He will judge between the nations and will settle the disputes for many people. They will beat their swords into ploughshares and their spears into pruning hooks. Nation will not take up sword against nation, nor will they train for war anymore.'

Peace comes, nations are exalted, everyone is blessed. Sounds good, doesn't it?

Recovering our mission

I was struck recently reading about the incredible missionary movement at the end of the nineteenth century. Here in Manchester, hundreds of young men and women were laying down their lives to take the gospel to the ends of the earth. I heard about a missionary meeting at Methodist Central Hall where people were invited to volunteer to go to a dangerous part of Africa with the good news – but warned that the average life expectancy of a missionary to this place was just sixteen weeks. That night the altar was literally crowded with young men and women willing to lay down their lives. On the back of this kind of amazing commitment, world evangelisation was in sight, as wave after wave of men and women went to the far ends of the earth. The church of Jesus was praying, planning, fundraising and sending out its best to fulfil the Great Commission.

Then, tragically, as the twentieth century dawned, mankind did the opposite of verse 4, beating our ploughshares into swords and our pruning hooks into spears. The same Christian nations who had sent out the missionaries, turned on one another in two terrible World Wars. The foot was taken off the gas of world missions.

Nowadays to say we should reach the whole world for Christ, and that he really is the only Saviour and Lord is usually seen as politically incorrect or a hopeless cause. But I'm going to say it and keep on saying it because I know he really is our only hope. We were created to be a 'going' people with a commission to take that message from the Lord himself to the estates of this nation and to the ends of the earth.

For the last 17 years I've dreamt that our Eden teams – going to the nation's tough communities often at great personal cost – could really play a small part in reigniting some of this missionary fire. I'm absolutely convinced that God spoke to me at the start of the whole Eden adventure through Psalm 37 and promised that 'the righteousness of the cause would shine like the noonday sun' (Psalm 37:6) which sounds a bit like verses 1-3 of Isaiah 2, 'and that the meek would inherit the land and enjoy great peace' (Psalm 37:11), which sounds a lot like verse 4. 'Bring it on, God!' is all I can say!

Finally, this little 'Mountain of the Lord' passage finishes with this charge: 'Come... let us walk in the light of the Lord.'

It's great to have big visions and dreams to take the gospel to the masses, and to have fantastic promises as we have from the Lord, but Isaiah reminds us that the key to seeing those big visions and dreams and the full measure of those promises fulfilled, is the daily business of walking in the light of the Lord – in other words, spending quality time with Jesus. We need to be those who seek to root out sin in our lives, be quick to forgive, love the unlovely, and continually lay down ourselves for the sake of Jesus. These and all the other spiritual disciplines we are learning about will mean that we will be in a place where God can use us to the max. And I want that with all my heart. What about you?

1. Think of the last time you felt 'on the back foot' in response to someone's criticism of your faith or the church. How did you feel? Defensive? Lost for words? Consider how you can give a humble, Christ-like response to critics next time you are in that situation.

2. Isaiah talks of the 'High Places' where false gods were worshipped in ancient times. What 'high places' of sin and idolatry are still present in your life? How will you remove them?

3. If revival is really ignited by personal cost, how much are you prepared to lay down for the mission of God? What could that look like for you this year? For example, have you ever considered joining an incarnational Eden team, moving your family to an impoverished urban neighbourhood in order to live out the gospel there?

1. Talking with Tristan when he said he thinks God is unfair in that he reveals himself in different degrees to different people.

   I now think that although Tristan thinks he is open-minded, in fact he has his foot against the door. I might challenge him on that.

2. – Disobedience over drinking alcohol.
   – Idolatry over size of congregation.
   – Thought-life.

   They need to be removed by throwing myself on God's mercy + asking for his forgiveness + strength to repent.

3. Not yet enough. I need to have more courage to ask people to step forward.

   I (we) could invite a youth worker to come + live in the vicarage.

PRAYER

Lord, I am challenged when I consider
what you laid down for me.
I am humbled by your love for me
and your great compassion for the lost, the lonely
and the unloved of this world.
Teach me more today about your plans
for my part in your mission.
Help me to be willing to lay down
what you ask of me and to be obedient
to every aspect of your call.
Teach me how to come to you
and then be sent out by you.

Amen

STORY: FAMILY VALUES

Multiplication is at the heart of The Message. Since the earliest days of The Tribe, we've had a vision to send missionaries carrying the DNA of The Message right across the country and beyond. We've trained hundreds of young evangelists through our Academy training programme and we've sent out Associate ministries with our backing and blessing.

MESSAGE ACADEMY: INVESTING IN THE NEXT GENERATION

The Message is all about multiplication: multiplication of disciples and multiplication of mission. That's why over the last thirteen years, we've made investing in the next generation of youth evangelists a core part of our life and ministry. What started out as Xcelerate became Genetik and is today's Message Academy. Through them all, we've trained well over 200 youth workers and creative evangelists. Many have gone on to serve churches, start new ministries, or lead their own creative missions teams.

For Prisons Team Leader Tim Mycock, who actually became a Christian when the World Wide Message Tribe visited his school, Xcelerate provided Tim with a strong foundation for the calling he would go on to pursue: 'God had broken my heart for young people and I knew youth work was going to be part of my future. But aside from volunteering with my church and at Message events, I wasn't sure what that was going to look like. Xcelerate helped me see it.

'We had teaching in everything – lots of doctrine and theology as well as practical youth work stuff. Even now, lads will ask me questions and I'll find myself recalling teaching I had then that has stuck. I got exposure to a lot of the practical stuff of working with the poor and those on the margins – learning about issues like homelessness and what agencies there are and how they connect.'

Xcelerate gave Tim a bigger vision of what God is doing among the poor and how his people can join in: 'I realised on Xcelerate that our job is to advance the Kingdom of heaven and as part of that, to see people coming to Christ. I learned that every time we speak truth, every time we serve the poor, every time we love the unlovable, it's a breakthrough of the Kingdom.'

When the original 'Message in Prisons' (now Reflex) team formed to respond to work with the North West's young offenders, Tim was a natural choice for their first prisons outreach and resettlement worker. And after more than ten years in the role, Tim took over leadership of the team which works in four prisons and young offenders' institutions.

Jamie Hill, Message Missions Director, comments about Message Academy: 'Academy is without doubt the very best year-out programme I've ever been involved with. The mix of teaching, hands-on experience and exposure to what God's up to through The Message is second to none. I say to church leaders everywhere: send us your best and we'll send them back better – more alive and ready to go.'

LIGHT: TAKING IT TO THE 'NEXT LEVEL'

Light launched in 2011 as a new home for LZ7 and as a platform for a new wave of ministries aiming to shine the light of the gospel into the mainstream music scene. One of the members of The Tribe's final line-up, Lindz West developed the ministry of LZ7 while here at The Message, taking the band to the top of the bill at festivals and even into the mainstream charts across Europe. Today Light are still part of The Message family and are more focussed than ever on getting their music in front of millions of young people, but they're also committed to developing a better way for those who make responses to Christ at gigs to grow as Christians.

Lindz explains: 'We did 65 schools gigs last year and, no disrespect to the churches, but not one of them had anything credible to take away at the end of the night. Some gave away tracts, others whole Bibles, and inevitably you would find piles of them in the bins at the end of the night. The question was, how can we develop something that kids find really valuable and they want to go back to when they get home?'

The AAA Pass is Light's groundbreaking response – a free lanyard giving access to online resources which Lindz describes as a 'next-level discipleship course'. Young people who respond at LZ7 gigs or events are presented with an AAA pass on a lanyard with a scratch-off key code on the reverse. The code gives them access to a website, theAAApass.com, which opens with a presentation of the 4 Points and continues to a 9-step discipleship programme called living4God.net, presented by Lindz, LZ7 bandmate Remi, Twelve24's Josh and Ryan, Charlie Blyth from A21/Hillsong and rapper Guvna B.

At each stage the resource is loaded with downloads, exclusive tracks and videos, but front and centre is an accessible, step-by-step introduction to the gospel, the church, the Bible and prayer, and topics including forgiveness and justice. Living4God can also be used in the context of a 9-week Alpha-style youth course, meeting in a Starbucks or another neutral venue as a follow-up to a schools week.

The fact that the AAA Pass is an online resource means that not only are there multiple entry points – kids can access the material via a computer or any phone – it also means that it can be updated with the latest songs and videos. There's also the potential to tailor the AAA Pass city by city, opening up the possibility of linking kids to specific churches and youth workers.

But perhaps the most exciting feature of the AAA Pass is that it's possible to track accurately how many people are engaging with the material and – crucially – how many are making it through to the end. In

THE AAA PASS

a recent pilot of the resource in Slough, says Lindz, the results were astonishing: 'A thousand kids came to the end of week gig and we gave out 600 passes. Of these, 479 went through the whole course – we know because we could see how many had logged on with their pass.'

The band launched the AAA Pass with a huge giveaway of AAA Pass lanyards at the 2014 Big Church Day Out. With a massive audience through schools and festivals at home and abroad – the band estimate they have played to 750,000 young people over the last two years – the resource could be a catalyst for a huge amount of serious discipleship. The Message and Light are also gearing up to make the AAA Pass a central part of the national schools tour, 'Illuminate Your City' we are planning for 2015.

'I'd love to see a tipping point happening,' says Lindz. 'More young people engaging with Jesus, resourcing the church in an incredible way. People are looking at this and calling it a game changer – that's my dream for it.'

We at The Message are so excited by what we've seen from Lindz and the Light guys since they became Associates back in 2011. Not only are they breaking new ground with the size of the platforms they're on, but they're working hard at the really important stuff – not just counting hands but making disciples. The AAA pass is a big step forward in bringing together the technology every young person loves to use and the life-changing message of discipleship they need to hear.

LZ7 PERFORM AT EO FESTIVAL 2012, NETHERLANDS

THE SONG
OF THE
VINEYARD

CHAPTER FIVE

I will sing for the one I love
    a song about his vineyard:
my loved one had a vineyard
    on a fertile hillside.
He dug it up and cleared it of stones
    and planted it with the choicest vines.
He built a watchtower in it
    and cut out a winepress as well.
Then he looked for a crop of good grapes,
    but it yielded only bad fruit.
'Now you dwellers in Jerusalem and people of Judah,
    judge between me and my vineyard.
What more could have been done for my vineyard
    than I have done for it?
When I looked for good grapes,
    why did it yield only bad?
Now I will tell you
    what I am going to do to my vineyard:
I will take away its hedge,
    and it will be destroyed;
I will break down its wall,
    and it will be trampled.
I will make it a wasteland,
    neither pruned nor cultivated,
    and briers and thorns will grow there.
I will command the clouds
    not to rain on it.'
The vineyard of the Lord Almighty
    is the nation of Israel,
and the people of Judah
    are the vines he delighted in.
And he looked for justice, but saw bloodshed;
    for righteousness, but heard cries of distress.

Isaiah 5:1-7

Who is your lover?

The Song of the Vineyard at the start of Isaiah 5 has been called a literary masterpiece, virtually peerless among ancient writings, particularly in the original Hebrew with its brilliant use of language and wordplay. But the truth is, there is something in here for everyone – even if your preferred reading matter is more The Sun than Shakespeare!

Isaiah, as we've discovered, is a big book in so many ways, but it's also a rollercoaster book, going from doom and gloom, woes and judgements to glorious encounters and ecstatic revelation, chapter by chapter. In a sense, this is a tension we all live with on a daily basis as we simultaneously experience all the rubbish going on around us, while clinging on to the amazing future we've been promised. The 'what is' against the 'what will be', if you like.

This can be especially hard when you are living with the kind of promises we are at The Message Trust. As I've explained already, at the start of this whole adventure I know God spoke to me in my bedroom from that famous passage in Isaiah 43 and promised us that he was ready to do 'a new thing' with 'rivers in the desert and streams in the wasteland', plus I had the nearest thing to my own Isaiah 6 moment in a car park, minutes after speaking for the first time publically about Eden. Again God brought us some amazing revival promises from Psalm 37, that 'he will make your righteous reward shine like the dawn, your vindication like the noonday sun' (v.6) and that we would 'enjoy peace and prosperity' (v.11). Sometimes we feel a long way from these promises after more than 25 years of hard graft, but as I reflect, I can indeed see the trickle becoming a stream and am ready for the mighty river of blessing when God sees fit. Come on, Lord!

In Isaiah 5 this tension is evident almost verse by verse. The chapter starts with 'I will sing for the one I love, a song about his vineyard'. In Isaiah's day the end of the grape harvest was a time for one heck of a party, with lots of food, drink and entertainment. Often random people would get up and entertain the revellers with a song or a dance, open-mic style. Isaiah decided he was going to use this opportunity to bring a song to his unsuspecting audience. Not only is it a powerful prophetic word, but also a severe warning from none other than God himself. In many ways this is what the bands and theatre companies we deploy are doing. Fulfilling their calling and doing something very similar – they are going into the public space and bringing the word of the Lord through the creative arts.

In the song, the prophet's lover is the Lord. This got me thinking: 'Is the Lord my Lover? Not just my Saviour, Friend, Comforter and Lord, but my Lover too?' Being a lover speaks to me of passion, of life and of intimacy. I read recently that GK Chesterton wrote in his biography of Francis of Assisi, 'His religion was not a thing like a theory but a thing like a love affair.' Is there any higher compliment that could be paid to a man? Sometimes I know my faith, even with all my loud preaching and arm waving is far from a love affair. It can easily become passionless and cold, where once it really did burn. It also made me think, 'God, please give us some more wacky, fanatical nutty Jesus lovers at The Message who I have to calm down a bit because they are so passionate!'

A bumper harvest

Isaiah says his lover had a vineyard and, verse 2, 'He dug it up and cleared it of stones and planted it with the choicest vines. He built a watch tower in it and cut out a wine press as well.' In other words, he cared for the vineyard, gave it his attention, did everything that was necessary for a massive harvest – yet 'it only yielded bad fruit.'

These words are undoubtedly for two horizons. Yes, they are for God's chosen people whom he had poured his love on and rescued again and again and who were given everything in order to show the world what he's like. But almost 3,000 years later, they apply to us, too. Look how much the Lord has given his church! Of course he has given his very Son for us and poured his Spirit into our lives. We've got the Bible in innumerable translations, great teachers, wonderful worship leaders, more financial resources than any generation in history. All he wants is some good fruit – the very thing we were chosen and appointed to do in the first place according to Jesus (John 15:16). Surely that is not too much to ask?

The scary thing is that Isaiah makes it quite clear that if the vineyard he's cared for continually produces no fruit, or even worse bad fruit, then he will actively *remove* his blessing: 'Now I will tell you what I am going to do to my vineyard: I will take away its hedge, and it will be destroyed; I will break down its wall, and it will be trampled. I will make it a wasteland, neither pruned nor cultivated, and briers and thorns will grow there. I will command the clouds not to rain on it' (v.5-6).

How scary these verses are. Especially as they actually describe the place that many Christians and churches are at where they are going through the motions but to one degree or the other 'the glory of the Lord has departed.'

It can so easily happen if we don't guard our lives against those things that Isaiah warns us of in the rest of the chapter – such as being greedy and grabbing more for ourselves while living in a world of need (v.8) or drinking too much and partying too hard (v.11-12) or being clever in our own eyes and wise in our own sight (v.21). Ouch!

So let's allow the Holy Spirit to examine us – and this song that he inspired Isaiah to sing all those years ago to convict us, and if there is anything in our lives that could stop us becoming the bumper-fruit people God has planned for us to be, let's kick it out, mercilessly.

REFLECTION

1. How do you feel about the Lord being your lover? Does that word make you feel uncomfortable, safe, secure or 'on edge'? St. Dimitri of Rostov wrote, 'No unity with God is possible without an exceeding great love.' Loving and joining go together. Examine those first few verses again, asking the Holy Spirit to reveal new truths to you about your own walk with God.

2. Would you describe yourself as a nutty, passionate follower of Jesus? Or have you changed since your conversion and become more polite, safe and conventional in your attitudes and actions? All of us need to heed the challenges of Isaiah to maintain intimacy with God. What would reignite some of the old flames within you? Perhaps you could pray for God to show you today.

3. No one wants to bear bad fruit as a believer. Can you detect anything on the vine of your life that God would find unsavoury? Take some time out to read Psalm 51 and meditate on its truths for you.

1. I want the Lord to be my lover!

   Give me more passion, God!

2. I have become more 'careful', more reserved, + less likely to champion Jesus.

3. Yes, my fear of upsetting some people in the church means I hold back from making changes which might need to be made.

   Yes! My unbelief when people talk of incredible things that God has done.

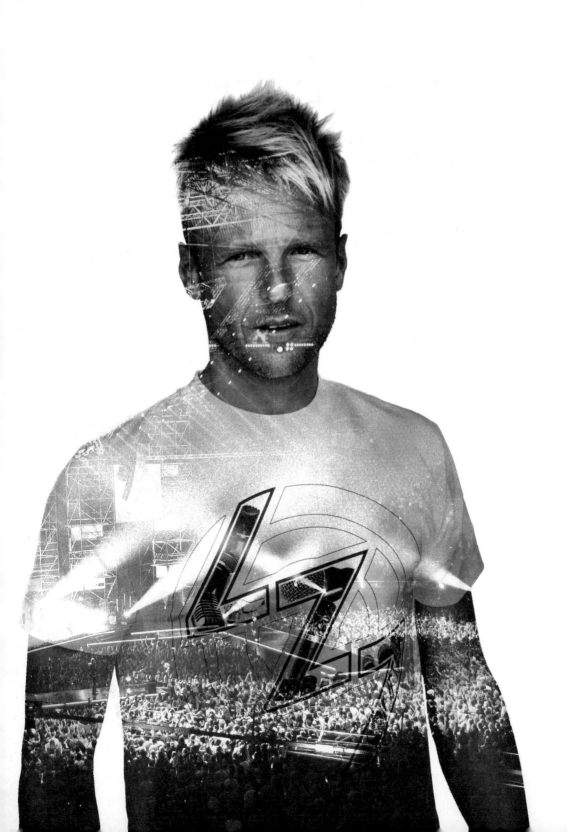

PRAYER

Lord,
I want to be someone who bears bumper
harvests of fruit for you.
Please help me to know
all I need to know in order to do that.
Keep me from a safe, quiet and boring life
and help me to radically fulfil
your great commission for me
as I go into the world.
Help me to encounter you today
not just as my Lord,
but as the lover of my soul.

Amen

TESTIMONY
LAUREN JUBB

'I've seen God move
so much, incredible
transformation'

Lauren's life has been impacted in several ways by the Message: she was first reached by an Eden team, heard the gospel at a schools gig and most recently, graduated from the Message Academy. After winning the 2014 Urban Hero of the Year award, she announced she was applying to join an Eden team.

t's so important that we do whatever it takes to show young people that God loves them. If no one had taken the time to show me, I don't know where I'd be now.

I grew up in a home with a mum who was really poorly and a dad who walked out when I was seven. Even though I knew my mum loved me with all her heart, I never felt very loved – I always felt like the loose end, really rejected. By the time I was a teenager, I was angry with the world, angry with anything that came at me. I thank God for my foster parents who were strong Christians, and the Eden Arbourthorne team who knew exactly what I was like back then. They prayed for me and were always so supportive, sticking by me when I was an angry young girl, a real challenge to work with.

It was at an LZ7 gig where I first encountered God's love in my heart. I was 15, having loads of fun, just jumping about with my friends. When Lindz started talking about God's love for me, it really stopped me in my tracks. The kind of life I'd had up to that point, I thought that either there was no God, or if there was a God, he must hate me. But in Lindz's words I just heard my own story. He was describing exactly how I was

feeling. I wanted what he was taking about, that love and unconditional acceptance, because I hadn't known too much of that in my own life. Up to that point, I used to feel like I was never accepted. I used to feel like I was really ugly and no one ever really liked me.

When you feel that way, and then you discover what God actually says about you and how he loves you, and that what you've always believed is not the truth at all – that's incredible. It changes your life. You suddenly realise, I want every girl to know this. I want everyone who's ever felt that way about themselves to know the truth. They are amazing. They are created beautiful.

The Eden team were incredible. When I became a Christian and decided to follow God, they were really supportive. They helped me to understand God more and understand the Bible more. They helped me find a mentor and they gave me so much support. They were there from day one, never giving up on me. Eden showed me a love that nothing can compare to.

When your life's been changed in that way, that's what you want to do for other people. You start to believe with all your heart that God's going to change their life, too. You believe that people working alongside them are going to help change their life. God is a God of transformation. You want to scream it from the mountaintops.

So I started volunteering with the Eden team, helping out in a youth group, with computer games and dance and stuff. Then I got asked to help out in a girls group, teaching them more about the

Bible and what God said about them. That was great – I knew a lot of the girls already so it was really natural and real. All this time, God was healing me and restoring me. I chose not to let my past overtake me, but to overtake my past. One day my Eden team leader told me about the Message Academy course and said I should apply for it. I think I thought I knew what Message Academy was going to be all about. I assumed it would be a year of youth work like I was used to doing in Sheffield. How wrong could I be! The first two terms in particular felt like God dealing with all the issues in me. What I've discovered is the more I've grown in my character, the more God's been able to use me to help others. This year has been the best year I've ever had. What Message Academy has also done is to help me find my calling. I know I'm called to work with young people. It seems to me like a massive privilege to get alongside young people and talk to them about God, to get to see them open up and grow.

I've seen God move so much this year, some incredible transformation. On one of my placements with the Eden Bus we met a group of three girls who were really hard work – in fact they came right out and told us they hated us. That's really challenging when all you want to do is show them God loves them. But what I've learnt is you have to stick with it. My Eden team never gave up on me – so why should I give up on the young people I'm working with? So we stuck it out, kept working with them and showing them we loved them. I shared my story with them, about where I've been and where I am now. One of the girls in particular could really relate to my story. By the end of the year, we saw all three of them commit their lives to Jesus.

It's amazing how God has used my personal story to impact so many lives for good. They can relate to the pain, and when I show them the way out of the pain – knowing God's love, beginning to trust in Jesus – they want to take it too.

My life is a story of transformation. My whole outlook has changed. I know I am beautiful, I'm created for a purpose, I'm me for a reason. My relationship with my mum is so much better. I know I have a purpose and a destiny. And it's all because someone did whatever it took to show me God's love.

HERE I AM...
SEND ME!

CHAPTER SIX

ISAIAH 6:1-8

In the year that King Uzziah died, I saw the Lord, high and exalted, seated on a throne; and the train of his robe filled the temple. Above him were seraphim, each with six wings: with two wings they covered their faces, with two they covered their feet, and with two they were flying. And they were calling to one another:

'Holy, holy, holy is the Lord Almighty;
   the whole earth is full of his glory.'

At the sound of their voices the doorposts and thresholds shook and the temple was filled with smoke.

'Woe to me!' I cried. 'I am ruined! For I am a man of unclean lips, and I live among a people of unclean lips, and my eyes have seen the King, the Lord Almighty.'

Then one of the seraphim flew to me with a live coal in his hand, which he had taken with tongs from the altar. With it he touched my mouth and said, 'See, this has touched your lips; your guilt is taken away and your sin atoned for.'

Then I heard the voice of the Lord saying, 'Whom shall I send? And who will go for us?'

And I said, 'Here am I. Send me!'

Isaiah 6:1-8

Jesus on the throne

I saiah 6 is perhaps the most famous passage in Isaiah and one of the most well-known and loved in the whole Bible. In many ways you might have expected Isaiah to *start* his book with this chapter. After all it is his testimony; the reason he has the authority to write this book in the first place. But I guess that he didn't because he had learnt a lesson that all of us who preach need to learn – the message is so much more important than the messenger.

As Isaiah sits praying in the temple, the Lord arrives in all his glory on an enormous and majestic throne surrounded by worshipping angelic beings. This is not just any 'Lord' but our Lord – Jesus, himself, as we shall one day see him. If you have any doubts about this, John made it very clear in John 12:41 that Isaiah saw Jesus' full glory here. Hundreds of years before he was born in Bethlehem, Jesus was on his throne ruling over the world. Hebrews 1:8 says about Jesus, 'Your throne, O Lord, will last for ever and ever.' I don't know how anybody can say that the Bible is unclear about Jesus' deity. Jesus is God! The Bible is so patently clear about it and we should be, too. Jesus is God and the whole world needs to know it!

The reality of heaven

Isaiah got a glimpse in that temple of the hidden world of heaven, a world that is just as real as the one we can see. All around us are angels and archangels, principalities and powers and maybe even the odd seraph – which literally means 'burning ones.' (Although seraphs are such rare creatures that this is the only mention of them in the entire Bible.)

My nephew Matthew joined our first Eden team to live on England's most deprived estate when he was seventeen years old. I remember him coming into work one day and saying, 'Andy, I've seen angels!' Apparently on his prayer walk he saw what he described as little burning ones sat on the roof of every Eden house, as though they were on guard to protect them. What a comfort and encouragement that was!

In the Bible these angels and other heavenly beings are our role models for worship. They were not just calling to the Lord but encouraging one another as they sing: 'Holy, Holy, Holy is the Lord Almighty, the whole earth is filled with his glory.' When we get together there needs to be a horizontal aspect to our worship as well as a vertical one. We are to spur one another on by our passion and desire for the Lord. We are also to look for the glory of the Lord everywhere, because the whole earth is filled with his train – not just our meetings!

Unclean lips

As all this worship went on in the temple, things got more than a little scary for Isaiah. The door posts shook, the temple filled with smoke and he genuinely thought he was a dead man. All he could think of saying was, 'Woe to me! ...I am ruined! For I am a man of unclean lips, and I live among a people of unclean lips.' He was suddenly aware of his lack of purity and holiness in that place of utter glory.

For five chapters Isaiah had pretty much been breathing fire and speaking woe to the Jewish people. But suddenly, in the presence of the majestic awesomeness of the Lord, the spotlight is on him and all he can find to say is 'I am unclean!'

He realises that it's not just Israel that is sinful but in light of the Lord's holiness, he is too. He is black with sin himself and in desperate need of a Saviour. This is the place we need to pray people get to, because without a genuine sense of our own sin-sickness, how can anyone truly turn to the only one who can heal them? One of the reasons I love our prisons work so much is that generally you don't need to convince the inmates either that they are sinners, or that they need a Saviour. They already know.

It is a sobering truth that one day everyone we will ever meet will be in that same position Isaiah found himself in, confronted by a Holy God. But unlike Isaiah, for so many it will be too late to receive forgiveness. Surely that's got to spur us on to get out there and tell some more people the life-changing good news! That the 'holy, holy, holy' one got down from his throne, came to earth, showed us what God is like, ultimately died on a cross and was punished for all the sins of all time, then rose again and conquered death once and for all. (I think I can feel a 'Hallelujah!' coming on!)

He is absolutely the only one worthy of saying this because of who he is and what he has done. He is the only one who has the right to say, 'Your guilt is taken away and your sins are atoned for.' We need to hear both of these things loud and clear. Our sins are forgiven and also our guilt is taken away. So many Christians are crippled by guilt because our friends the angels and archangels aren't the only ones watching us. The devil and his nasty minions are at work too. Their plan is to accuse us, condemn us and keep us in defeat, trapped by our past. We need to remember at all times that Jesus has forgiven us, chosen not to remember our sins and has a bright and triumphant future for us if we will co-operate with him.

Once you've got it – firstly a big vision of God, followed by a profound sense of your own unworthiness and then a real awareness of God's grace and forgiveness – there really is only one response to the cry from the throne of, 'Whom shall I send? And who will go for us?'

'Send me!' This is the reply that Isaiah gave. Whatever it means, whatever the cost, 'Here I am, send me!' How amazing would it be if we could see a new bunch of radical believers gripped by this invitation and shouting out their own heartfelt response?

1. In a world of political correctness, people refuse to accept that Jesus is not *a* way, *a* truth and *a* life, but *the* way. Have you had an encounter with someone where you have had to argue this amazing fact? How did it make you feel?

2. Have you ever had the privilege of seeing an angelic being, or sensing a supernatural power or gifting from God? What were the circumstances of that experience and what were the results?

3. Isaiah struggled with the depths of his own sinfulness when confronted with the perfection and glory of heaven. And yet, God chose him, cleansed him and sent him out. How does this pattern reflect your own journey with God? What were you like before he called you? In which areas have you changed? Who has he sent you to?

1. I have tried to argue that Jesus is the only way. It can be like telling a beggar where to find bread & he totally ignores you.

2. Singing in tongues on the Alpha Day Away.

3. It was all about me. Getting my own satisfaction.
   I'm now passionate about seeing the community transformed by the love of Christ.

   He has sent me to Southcote.

PRAYER

You might want to pray the following ancient prayer
attributed to St Ignatius Loyola (1491-1556)
which is still as poignant and relevant today
as it was thousands of years ago.

'Teach us, good Lord, to serve you as you deserve;
to give and not to count the cost;
to fight and not to heed the wounds;
to toil and not to seek for rest;
to labour and not to ask for any reward,
save that of knowing that we do your will.'

Amen

STORY: Message Enterprise Centre, the story so far...

Over a decade of working in the prisons around the North West has taught us two crucial things that have shaped the way we work.

The first thing is that there is an incredible hunger among the young men and women in our prison system for Jesus. Here, without doubt, is where you'll find our nation's most broken people. Here are people who, more often than not, already know they need a Saviour. Often you don't need to tell them they've done wrong; they know they have.

You just need to tell them about Jesus who can forgive their wrongs if they will truly repent. As a result, our teams are seeing hundreds of first-time commitments every year, and dozens of baptisms right there in prison.

As I've often said myself, if I'd grown up with the backgrounds and baggage that's all too common in our prisons and young offenders' institutions, I'd have probably ended up in one too. It's just simply not OK to write off these young men and women as beyond hope. We need to send in teams to love and to reach out to as many as possible. We need to step up our outreach on the wings, Alpha and discipleship courses and chaplaincy work.

The second thing, we've learned the hard way. And that's that no matter how much we hope and pray for a particular young person to stay on the right track when they come out of prison, if a prison leaver goes straight back to the same home town and the same circle of friends, without a job and with only a bare minimum of support, chances are they will eventually go back to their old ways.

It's one thing to hear about the costs of reoffending – estimates suggest every unemployed ex-offender costs the taxpayer at least £50,000 a year, taking into account unemployment benefits, health care, drug or alcohol treatment, policing, prison and probation services – but it's quite another to see the destructive effects for yourself. It broke our hearts to see it, but time and time again we saw how young people we had introduced to Jesus would end up back in trouble, back before the courts and, all too often, back inside. The 'revolving door' of prison really does exist, and people we cared about were getting stuck in it. After long enough of watching this happen, we decided enough was enough. Someone had to do something. And by God's grace, we decided we would have a go.

The Message Enterprise Centre started as a pragmatic response to the problem of youth reoffending. We knew we needed to offer better answers to the questions of unemployment, poor housing and destructive relationships for ex-offenders. These young men and women who had found new lives in Christ now needed a helping hand to start new lives in the community.

The idea of creating a business hub in the vacant and dilapidated warehouse next to our Sharston HQ seemed to fit the bill perfectly: it could act as an incubator for new businesses which would train and create jobs for young men and women, our Apprentices. Working with our Eden teams, we imagined placing them in homes where they could receive support and friendship outside of work hours, help with sorting out out a personal budget and getting on top of the stuff we all need to know: paying taxes, taking care of yourself. And in partnership with local churches, we dreamt of giving them a Christian mentor to disciple them, to ensure they were growing in faith and character.

Looking back, it seems nothing short of miraculous that during all these years, through housing boom and bust, the 20,000 square foot premises stayed vacant. It is as if they were earmarked for us. And at the right time, the Council accepted favourable terms, everything went through, and we collected the keys. There was a huge amount to be done – my first impression on seeing the inside of the warehouse was that it reminded me of The Day of the Triffids – but it was great to be offering work straight away to young men who cleared the site and got it ready for the builders coming in. Even two of those guys committed their lives to Christ!

The building was designed as a fit-for-purpose facility containing three street-level shop premises, an office home for two or three other businesses, meeting and training rooms and extra office space to rent out. Having selected our contractor, TJM Projects, work began on the site in May 2012 with a target end date of November 2012 and a projected cost of £1.3 million. The site was boarded up and sealed ahead of demolition of the roof and most of the external walls. Building work began and ended on time and on budget. That in itself is a miracle in this day and age.

Praise God, the Message Enterprise Centre was officially opened in January 2013 by the Chief Constable of Greater Manchester, Sir Peter Fahy. A firm supporter of the project from the beginning, Sir Peter warmly endorsed the MEC, calling it 'a massive opportunity for prison leavers to transform their lives and a massive saving for society in general.'

We launched with four enterprises 'open for business' – a café and catering firm, a hair & beauty salon, a cycle recycling shop and property maintenance and development business. Since then Wedding Angels has also opened onsite, organising weddings and training young women in dressmaking and alterations.

The goal of each business is both sustainability and discipleship. We're committed to working hard, building up our clients and growing our turnover (we're also serious about paying fair wages and bonuses for hitting targets, by the way). But our mission priority is to help young people learn skills, a work ethic and the value of contributing to a team and to society. So there's a careful balance to be struck and our team of business managers and mentors are doing amazingly at blazing a trail where as far as we know, no one's gone before.

If you take a look at our city, entrepreneurial talent is everywhere to be seen. And you don't have to go to business school to be an entrepreneur – there are plenty of them doing shady deals out of BMWs around our needy neighbourhoods. Imagine harnessing the entrepreneurial energy of guys like that into setting up chains of 'Shine Hair & Beauty' or 'Mess Cafés' around the city. I do. All the time.

Which brings me to our amazing Apprentices. There are two of our Apprentices' testimonies in this book, and that's no accident – very often our Apprentices have the most harrowing and the most hope-inspiring stories of anyone we work with.

Jason (page 42) was our first apprentice. He started work with our building business even before the MEC opened its doors. Before coming to the MEC, Jason had 12 years of prison behind him, and he'd never worked for more than two weeks in his life. But straight away, under the wing of Dominic, our building Business Manager, he found a supportive mentor who was as committed to his progress as to making a profit. Jason is thriving, describing himself as a 'tree that's come into the light':

'It's been amazing coming into work every day and just getting on with the job. I've got a purpose. I meet loads of people who spend their time saying, "I can't wait to finish work". But to be honest, I love my job. I know that God's got me there for a reason. I like to see the change – seeing the old run-down things brightened up, being made new. Just like myself.'

And then there's Amy (pictured right, and on page 111). Meeting her now, you would never imagine the violent past Amy who works in our hair and beauty salon has had. She's been utterly transformed by the power of God. She won our Urban Hero of the Year award in 2013

and I'll never forget her words to the 800-odd great and good at the Reebok Stadium that year: 'This is Jesus's award... none of us would be here if it weren't for him. Thank you, Jesus.'

You could say the same for her colleague Laura, who shares her story of radical healing on page 126 – and with anyone in Shine who'll care to listen! Here again is a story of a life that had hit the buffers until Jesus rescued it. Mired in addiction, a series of abusive relationships behind, Laura is freed from it all and now looking ahead to a future with a husband and reunited with her son. I could mention many more, powerful testimonies to the life-changing power of the gospel that we hear week by week.

I love the way that God so often brings us back to where we started so we can look back and marvel at what he's accomplished through us. To me it's no coincidence that what started 25 years ago with a factory, a lot of Lady Diana braces and leather ties, and a workforce of unruly young men is today seeing the same kinds of lads – and girls – beautifully saved and becoming all God's made them to be. Although we could have never imagined all this, the heart is still the same. The seeds we sowed in tears back in the beginning have grown and we are reaping an amazing joyful harvest today.

This is what motivates us to keep going – and believe me, there have been plenty of moments where it would have been easier to give up. There really is nothing like hearing another dramatic story of someone whose life has gone from being utterly messed up to being completely turned around.

And with our Apprentices, we're not just talking about praying a prayer and keeping their heads down. These men and women are so often on fire for Christ. They're leading others to know him. They're testifying to his goodness day after day at work. And they're actively looking for ways to 'go', to reach others in his name and do great things in their own right.

We love the fact that God changes lives at The Message. No life is too broken for God to put it back together again. And not just to save them, but to send them.

APPRENTICES AT WORK

ARE WE NICER THAN GOD?

CHAPTER SEVEN

ISAIAH 6:8-13

Then I heard the voice of the Lord saying, "Whom shall I send? And who will go for us?"

And I said, "Here am I. Send me!" He said, "Go and tell this people:

"'Be ever hearing, but never understanding;
    be ever seeing, but never perceiving.'

Make the heart of this people calloused;
    make their ears dull
    and close their eyes.
Otherwise they might see with their eyes,
    hear with their ears,
    understand with their hearts,
and turn and be healed."

Then I said, "For how long, Lord?"

And he answered:

"Until the cities lie ruined
    and without inhabitant,
until the houses are left deserted
    and the fields ruined and ravaged,
until the Lord has sent everyone far away
    and the land is utterly forsaken.
And though a tenth remains in the land,
    it will again be laid waste.
But as the terebinth and oak
    leave stumps when they are cut down,
    so the holy seed will be the stump in the land.'"

Isaiah 6:8-13

Encounter with God

I'm no Isaiah, but as I've already written in this book, there have been some awesome moments in my life when I know that Almighty God has spoken to me in specific ways. I have known times where I have felt him asking me the same question he asked of Isaiah in chapter 6, verse 8: 'Whom shall I send? And who will go for us?' Maybe you have, too.

I wrote in the Introduction about the moment God spoke to me from Isaiah 43, right back at the beginning of the whole Message adventure and we embarked on launching Manchester's biggest ever youth mission, with the promise of 'streams in the desert and rivers in the wasteland.'

And I mentioned another encounter with the Lord when at the start of Eden, he spoke words from Psalm 37 to us in a Manchester car park. He told us so clearly that if his people would start to plant themselves in some of Britain's toughest estates he would move and bring change and healing. Even more recently, God has miraculously brought Isaiah 60 to my attention through various different sources with the promise that he is about to do all of the above and swiftly!

As an organisation I believe it is fair to say that on the back of God speaking like this, we have sought to answer him with a cry of 'Here I am, send me!' and tried our best to be obedient to what he was calling us to.

Hard hearts

I do, however, wonder if we would have been so keen to respond if the message we had been given was the kind of message Isaiah received on the back of his mega temple encounter! The Lord told him to go and tell the people of Israel and warn them that because of their sin and rebellion, massive judgement was coming their way. That is not an easy message to carry, but Isaiah takes up this scary responsibility.

The Lord says in verse 10, 'the people's hearts will be hardened, or calloused.' This is what God saw. This is what he knew to be true and this is what Isaiah had to pass on. His judgement started because of people being hardened to his message. I am sure you can identify with his assessment of his nation. Our own society is equally full of sinful, self-absorbed people, not helped by what often appears to be a largely prayerless, weak and ineffective church.

People's hearts are hard to God. Evangelism is difficult. The church is boring. Christians fight with one another and the average person sees religion or relationship with God to be unimportant, and has little or no interest in spiritual things. But we know that this is not the whole story. Even in the midst of such rebellion, sin and selfishness, God is not passive or silent. He is still on the move and as 2 Chronicles 16:9 says, he is looking for faithful people: 'For the eyes of the Lord range throughout the earth to strengthen those whose hearts are fully committed to him.'

Hard times

Frighteningly, the Lord goes on to explain to Isaiah that for Israel their behaviour and lack of obedience will lead to utter devastation. It's like the sentence has been passed in heaven and Isaiah's prophecy will put that into effect. Is it any wonder that Isaiah asks in verse 11, 'For how long, Lord?' It is interesting to note that the Lord doesn't really give him a specific answer. He just replies with a phrase: 'until it's all been accomplished.'

We know that Isaiah had to keep up his role of God's prophet of gloom and doom for around 40 years, as, in horror, he had to watch everything he was prophesying coming to pass. Only in Isaiah 40, written some 40 years later, was he able to say to the Lord's people that comfort was coming and that their hard service had been completed.

During those 40 years I'm sure he had to remind himself again and again of this encounter with the Lord in the temple. When the going gets tough and the calling is hard, it's good for us to remind ourselves of why we are standing strong. In the midst of a battle season, we need to remind our souls of the times in the past when the Lord spoke to us and allow those times to fuel our gutsy persistence.

Nicer than God?

Journeying through the first few chapters of Isaiah has really got me thinking. Are we sometimes, as Gerald Coates has put it, 'nicer than God'? Of course our God is all-loving and full of mercy but he is also a holy and fearful judge who must therefore punish sin.

I remember that when I committed my life to Christ over forty years ago, I was given a classic tract called 'Journey into Life' (written in 1964 by Norman Warren, and still published today). Inside there was a picture of a coin with two sides that sought to represent the two sides of God's character. One side said 'love' and the other side said 'justice.' It's so crucial that we hold an understanding of God's love and God's justice in balance.

If we just teach the 'love' side of the coin, we end up with a distorted, weak gospel. Why? Because without God being holy, perfect and demanding justice, Jesus would not have had to die. Jesus died on the cross to face the full judgement and wrath that we deserved, in the face of a holy, perfect God.

Now of course love will always have the last word. But we need to remember that so-called 'gentle Jesus, meek and mild' spoke more about Hell than he did about Heaven. Why? Because he didn't want anyone to go there! His life was one great rescue mission, both from hellish lives now and from the penalty of Hell in the future. That same Jesus who classically said in John 3:16 'For God so loved the world that he gave his one and only Son....' also said a few verses later in John 3:36 'Whoever believes in the Son has eternal life, but whoever rejects the Son will not see life, for God's wrath remains on them.' We like one of those quotes a lot more than the other don't we? But both are equally true.

It was this sense of saving people from God's righteous wrath and judgement that sent so many missionaries from the UK to travel all over the world. But it was with a heart of love and the gospel message of good news that they walked in, too.

Our job is not to be gloomy, sour-faced miseries telling people what sinners they are, but to be a people blown away by what we're been saved from and committing ourselves with total abandon to playing our part in God's great rescue mission.

REFLECTION

1. Have you ever heard God reveal something powerful to you that sustained you in harder times? What was it, and what impact did that revelation have on you and others?

2. Do you sometimes find it hard to remember the two sides of God's character that I mentioned earlier? What aspects of your witness to others feel 'one-sided'? What could you do to redress the balance?

3. Can you recall what you have been saved from? What are you like now? Perhaps take some time to praise God for rescuing you.

1. Yes, at the retreat in Wales he revealed that he has me in the palm of his hand, & that Jesus is my friend.

2. No. I think I hold them in a healthy balance.

3. Yes. From self-centredness. Materialism. I am more peaceful, joyful, forgiving.

I love you. I worship you. I praise you.

PRAYER

Father,
thank you that you are a God of justice,
but also that you are slow to anger
and abounding in love.
Please help me to remember both sides
of your nature as I live out my faith in you
before friends and family.
Help me to honour the words
and revelation you have spoken to me.
Even if I have to wait 40 years
to see you move in one area,
help me to be found faithful in the waiting.

Amen

TESTIMONY
RYAN GRIGGS

'...all these things
followed a moment
of obedience'

Ryan Griggs is one third of Twelve24, one of our teams sharing the good news week in and week out in schools, prisons and communities. Like every member of our missions teams, he has his own story which connects powerfully with young people.

At 16 or maybe 17, I was definitely in a place where I was saying 'Here I am, send me.' I grew up without my dad but I was blessed that I still got fathered. Because I grew up in great church in the US, I had father figures all around me – my pastor, my youth leader, a couple other guys who really fathered me growing up. So I had this feeling that I wanted to serve God in some way to 'pay it back.'

It looked like I should probably train to be a pastor or something, so I started thinking about going to Bible college even though I was distinctly average in school and my heart wasn't in it.

Thing is, although I was too shy to say it, I actually wanted to be a rapper. I had grown up listening to bands like Cross Movement – hip-hop but with a message – ex-gangsters who had met Jesus and turned their lives around, using their music and their platform to reach people with the gospel.

But this was suburban Connecticut. I wasn't going to be a gangster. I grew up in a place called 'Country Place'! There were rougher spots but for the most part this was a nice area. Yeah, a lot of young guys I grew up with wanted to be rappers. But it didn't seem likely to happen to me.

Everybody needs a break, and mine came in church, of all places. My pastor had heard that me and this other guy had been rapping a little and so he basically told us to get up and rap in church one Sunday morning. He didn't give us much choice in the matter. So we did it, and it went off! People were crying, my mom and my brothers were amazed. Truth was, that was what I had always wanted to do, but I just didn't know that I could.

Amazingly I got introduced to a friend with connections to The Message Trust and The Band With No Name, and he encouraged me to apply to come to Manchester to train here. He showed me videos of what LZ7 and The Band With No Name were doing and said, 'Dude, you got to go to England. You could be in one of these bands – you've got to go.' To be totally honest, I had this whole Christian celebrity thing in my head. I thought: I'm going to go out there, get in a band. It's going to be sick. I'm going to be big!

Of course, God had bigger plans for me than that. I'd bought my plane ticket and three days before I was set to travel, I got a call from the Message office saying, 'Sorry, but the other rapper pulled out and we can't fund your track any more. You can still come but we're not going to teach you to rap any more.' This was the first sign that Genetik was going to be about much more than I expected at the start.

Being here in Manchester really challenged me to think for myself, read the Bible for myself and work out what I believed and why. And I grew up so much, so quickly. I began to see that most of all, God was after my character.

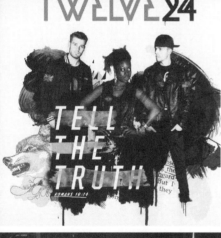

TWELVE24

TELL
THE
TRUTH

ROMANS 10:14

I clearly remember the first time I went out on the Eden Bus: I looked out the window into the car park and there was a group of maybe ten young people gathered round. In the middle there's the obvious leader, a 13-year-old kid with a girl on his lap, one hand clutching a Stella, the other hand down his pants. Another kid's handing a spliff round. I wanted to cry. How does this happen? And then it just clicked; the lights went on: These guys don't have dads. Or if they do, they're obviously not good dads, who can love them, tell them what's right and tell them when they're out of line.

That moment I knew why I was there. I felt it whenever we would go on the estates, on Eden projects. It meant that every time I rapped, I rapped with purpose as well as passion. I saw that I was able to personally mentor these guys, influence them, speak into their situations. In a way, I could be a father figure.

When we got a shot to form a new band in 2008, I was a different guy to the one who had landed in Manchester Airport the year before. I now felt more than called by God, I felt truly 'sent' by him. I had caught something that's in the atmosphere at The Message – a heart for the hardest-to-reach young people and a desire to show them Jesus, whatever the cost.

As a band we were totally inspired by The World Wide Message Tribe – both their passion for Manchester schools and the platform their music gave them. Our name, Twelve24, is a reference to John 12:24, where Jesus says, '…unless a kernel of wheat falls to the ground and dies, it remains only a single seed. But if it dies, it produces many seeds…' We are a multiplication of what The Tribe began. Our stories and our music are

what makes our schools weeks work, and they are the reason we always see young people becoming Christians at our concerts.

But just like The Tribe, we also want to get the 'lamp on a stand' and reach mass numbers through music and media. As well as going 'village to village' we feel like we've got to get up to the 'mountaintop.' We can't be in every school. We need a way to be in these kids' lives all the time. That's not physically possible, but it is possible through music and media. God has shown all of us in the band that fame is not the goal; getting the message out is the goal. We talk about being 'offensively obvious' with our message and we're not scared to say the name of Jesus.

The last seven years of my life have been an incredible journey. This band, what we've achieved so far, my ability to have a positive influence on thousands of kids, plus a whole load of other amazing stuff – my marriage, my church, my community… I realise that all these things followed a moment of obedience, a 'here I am, send me' moment.

FROM FEAR TO FAITH

CHAPTER EIGHT

When Ahaz son of Jotham, the son of Uzziah, was king of Judah, King Rezin of Aram and Pekah son of Remaliah king of Israel marched up to fight against Jerusalem, but they could not overpower it.

Now the house of David was told, 'Aram has allied itself with Ephraim'; so the hearts of Ahaz and his people were shaken, as the trees of the forest are shaken by the wind.

Then the Lord said to Isaiah, 'Go out, you and your son Shear-Jashub, to meet Ahaz at the end of the aqueduct of the Upper Pool, on the road to the Launderer's Field. Say to him, "Be careful, keep calm and don't be afraid. Do not lose heart because of these two smouldering stubs of firewood – because of the fierce anger of Rezin and Aram and of the son of Remaliah. Aram, Ephraim and Remaliah's son have plotted your ruin, saying, 'Let us invade Judah; let us tear it apart and divide it among ourselves, and make the son of Tabeel king over it.' Yet this is what the Sovereign Lord says:

"'It will not take place,
    it will not happen,
for the head of Aram is Damascus,
    and the head of Damascus is only Rezin.
Within sixty-five years
    Ephraim will be too shattered to be a people.
The head of Ephraim is Samaria,
    and the head of Samaria is only Remaliah's son.
If you do not stand firm in your faith,
    you will not stand at all.'"

Again the Lord spoke to Ahaz, 'Ask the Lord your God for a sign, whether in the deepest depths or in the highest heights.'

But Ahaz said, 'I will not ask; I will not put the Lord to the test.'

Isaiah 7:1-12

Twenty-Four-Seven, Three-Six-Five

The Message Trust is a faith ministry from start to finish. I don't want that only to be said of our early days, those crazy, heady days when we were acting like lunatics and pushing out on all fronts. I want that to be a living reality for today and for all time – we exist and we go forward by faith in Jesus Christ.

What we've learned over the years is that faith and fear are like two different operating systems. We all choose to operate in one or the other. Fear is our old operating system – fear of death, the future, our finances, our health, our relationships, fear of accusations against us. That's how we used to operate. But now we operate in the mindset of faith. We're a faith people. We're a people believing with confident faith that Jesus wins, and the Kingdom advances – faith that sees how this is all going to end: with millions coming to Christ, heaven being populated and Jesus being glorified.

But it's a choice. Every day and every hour we make that choice – which system are we going to live in?

Faith as a fuse and a filter

Reinhard Bonnke has a couple of great pictures of what faith is like. Firstly, he describes it as a fuse. Imagine all the incredible power of heaven waiting to be released on Manchester, on the tough estates, on the prisons as a 10,000 volts of electricity coming down a line from heaven. Yet there is a tiny little fuse, that the power needs to flow through – which is us. That small fuse makes all the difference. Can you see how vital it is to be a people of faith at a time like this?

He also calls faith a kind of immune system that filters out fears that would otherwise paralyse us. How can we worry about what's around the corner if we're remembering that if God is for us, who can be against us? (Romans 8:31).

How easily we can read these words and wonder, 'Is God for us? Is he really? I'm not sure I'm seeing the reality of that right now...' What more can God do to prove to you that he is for you? The living God invested everything so that you can be a man or woman of faith who partners with him to see people won for Jesus, the Kingdom come and heaven populated.

Trouble from all sides

Isaiah 7 shows us a man caught between fear and faith. King Ahaz is in trouble, from the left and from the right. He's got different invading armies coming from all sides, trying to take Jerusalem. It's been said that trouble comes in threes. We end up with multiple things to contend with at once, like many armies coming against us: maybe it is our health, or our debts, or our problems at work. Sometimes they all come at once. If and when that happens, what is our response going to be?

Ahaz's response was fear – he was 'shaken as the trees of the forest were shaken' (v2). Fear makes people do stupid things. Despite having all of God's promises, he starts to operate in fear. He ends up making a plan to make a pact with the foreign invaders.

To base important decisions on fear is a massive mistake, but it's one Christians can make all the time – fear of being alone gets us in trouble with bad relationships; fear of lack leads us to make poor financial decisions. It's a scary thing to present our plans to God and expect him to bless them, but how often we try to do just that – especially in the area of relationships. 'Yes, God, I know you've said don't go out with someone who's not a Christian and who doesn't share my passions, but here's my plan...' What a dangerous way to exist!

From fear to faith

In contrast to Ahaz's fear, we see Isaiah's impressive faith. We see him operating in peace, coming alongside the king to speak the word of the Lord to him: 'Be careful, keep calm and don't be afraid. Do not lose heart...' (v4).

What a lesson from God we have here: four ways to move from fear to faith, and they all start in the mind. Be careful – guard against those swings in your emotions. Choose to keep calm, and receive his peace. Choose not to be afraid. And do not lose heart – keep your heart strong, don't get disconnected from the Word and from fellowship.

Look closely at the text and you'll see that God sends Isaiah's son along with him, Shear-Jashub (v3). Isaiah was bringing up a boy in the Lord, passing on to him the mindset of faith. We all operate virally, every one of us. The Message Enterprise Centre and our Houses of Hope are viral environments, where faith can be caught. We're contagious people. What do you want to be contagious with: faith or fear?

I know what I want. I want anyone who spends any amount of time with me to come away feeling like their fuse has been reconnected, like their spiritual immune system has been built up, and they are ready to go again.

In good times and bad

Hebrews 11 is a chapter that has worked over the years to inspire me to greater and more contagious faith. It is full of men and women of God who operated like that fuse and witnessed power poured out through their life to bless the world. Abel, who was full of faith, Enoch who walked by faith, Noah whose family were saved by faith, Abraham whose faith took him away from his home and made him willing to even sacrifice his son; Isaac, Jacob, Joseph, Moses, Gideon... The list goes on.

But it also talks about a few whose faith led them into trouble. Jeremiah, who was beaten and imprisoned, Isaiah himself who we believe was sawn in half, and Zechariah who was stoned. Operating by faith will not necessarily mean that everything turns out rosy. Ten out of the 11 remaining apostles were horribly martyred. The way of faith is not an easy road. But it is the only road, the only road that counts as a life worth living.

Perhaps the greatest man of faith of all was the Apostle Paul. He made the greatest mark on this earth, planting churches and seeing extraordinary moves of the Spirit. In one sense we are only here because of that man's faithfulness as he carried the gospel out from Jerusalem. Written over Paul's faith journey was this amazing truth, 'Godliness, with contentment is great gain' (1 Timothy 6:6). Throughout his Christian life was the theme, 'I have learned to be content, whatever the circumstances' (Philippians 4:11).

There is an old saying that goes like this: 'I have everything I want, because I know what to want.' People of faith are people of contentment. And people who are content are rich, aren't they? What a thing it is to be as content in a slum as we would be in a palace. That's true faith in God.

REFLECTION

1. Can you think of anything that is causing you to operate in fear right now? Perhaps it could be your past, your health, finances, job situation or a relationship? List each thing that you are afraid of and ask God to help you to change your operating system in each circumstance from fear to faith. You may need to re-pray this prayer each time the fear tries to creep back into your mind. So keep praying it!

2. Isaiah's faith in the midst of trouble was both reassuring and impressive. What can your friends expect to hear when they come to you in times of difficulty? Are you encouraging and fearless or full of negativity and pessimism? Perhaps you could learn some Bible promises to speak over yourself and others when they are having a hard time.

3. A mark of Christian maturity is to be content with what God has blessed you with. Do you find it difficult to live in contentment? Do you always want the next phone or the newest upgrade of laptop? Do other people's possessions cause you to feel envious? Spend some time confessing this out loud to God and ask him for an upgrade in your own life, a spiritual understanding of contentment and gratitude for what you already have.

1. - People in church who don't like what we're doing.
   - Fear of running out of funds
   - Fear that prayer, rather than action, is a waste of time.

2. I am, at least, an optimist.

   Nothing can separate us from the love of Christ.

3. God has blessed me with so much. All I need comes from God.

PRAYER

Father God,
thank you for everything you give me.
Thank you for the gift of faith
which replaces fear in my life.
I ask that you would make me immune
to the fears that the enemy tries
to throw my way and remain plugged into
the power supply of your word.
Teach me today to be a positive
encouraging example to those around me
and to make others feel
they can be overcomers,
by the way I live
in contentment and peace.

Amen

'He's given
me everything
back that the
devil stole'

Laura is one of our amazing MEC apprentices who put a life of pain behind her when she accepted Christ. He has transformed her so much that to meet her today you'd never believe she was the same person. Laura was one of our 2014 Urban Hero Award winners, in recognition of her inspirational achievements.

If you come through the doors of Shine there is every chance you'll find me chatting away to a client as I cut or colour their hair. I trained to be a hairdresser years ago. But I can honestly say I am learning new things every day – about the never-ending goodness of God.

Two and a half years ago I knew my life really needed to change. I'd been a heroin addict for 17 years, on methadone for 13 years and on all sort of anti-depressants and anti-psychotic drugs. I was taking uppers to wake up, downers to go to sleep and other stuff to get through the day. Things got so bad that I was in a mental hospital with drug-induced psychosis, and my parents were told I would spend the rest of my life in there.

I was in and out of violent relationships and I was involved in all sorts of crime and theft to feed my drug habit. On top of all this, I'd had my son taken off me at 16 months old because I couldn't cope with being a mother at that point. I was even told I had a personality disorder. So I was trapped in a place of shame and guilt. Basically, my life was a mess. I got to the point where I got to thinking one of three things was going to happen – I would either kill myself, kill somebody else or be killed.

But it all changed one night – the night I heard about Jesus. It was in Scotland at an outreach being run by Victory Outreach. I was at my lowest point. I had nothing left. I was ill. My parents had told me they wanted nothing more to do with me. My son had been taken away from me. At this event I started hearing all these testimonies, one after another, about how Jesus had changed people's lives. People were testifying about being healed, one even testified to being healed from a personality disorder. So that night I made up my mind. I went to the front and said, 'If you can do it for these people, then please do it for me because I can't live like this any more.'

Within 12 hours I was on the Victory Outreach recovery programme in Manchester where I spent the next 18 months getting my life sorted out. The church runs a rehab with homes for men and women and a structured programme which gives people from broken backgrounds a new home and somewhere to belong. By the time I graduated God had done so much in me. He's set me free from drugs, healed me several times over and reconciled me with my family. I've now got a good relationship with my parents and at last I'm starting to get to know my son. This Christmas was the first Christmas I was able to spend at home with him since he was a baby and the first time I've ever seen him open his presents. I just thought, 'God, you've been so good to me.'

More than anything, it's been about getting closer to God who I believed could change my life. And he has. He's given me everything back that the devil stole from me. I hadn't worked as a hairdresser for years. Now he's given me a job doing what I love.

Shine is an amazing place. Business is growing and I'm getting the chance to be a mentor for the new apprentices coming through the salon. I feel like we're trailblazers, investing for the future. God knew exactly what he was doing when he brought me to The Message. I need people around me, a family to belong to, and that's what The Message has given me. I can be real with my managers and my colleagues here. This is a place of acceptance and belonging, where we're not judged for our faults but where we can encourage and support each other daily, and we can celebrate each other's growth.

God's using me, too. He's given me a real heart to reach out to people who don't know him who come into the salon. I can testify to his goodness. It's amazing to think that God could use someone like me to be a blessing to other people. I've shared my story at Prayer Days and at a business leaders' event in London. I want other people to hear me sharing my testimony and be asking God, 'if you can do it for her, will you do it for me too?'

If you'd told me a couple of years ago that all this would have changed, I'd have called you a liar because I never thought that could happen to me. I didn't think I was worthy of that. But if he can do all this within just two and a half years, what's he going to do with me in the future?

DECISIONS, DECISIONS

CHAPTER NINE

ISAIAH 7:13-9:7

The people walking in darkness
    have seen a great light;
on those living in the land of deep darkness
    a light has dawned.
You have enlarged the nation
    and increased their joy;
they rejoice before you
    as people rejoice at the harvest,
as warriors rejoice
    when dividing the plunder.

Isaiah 9:2-3

Three warnings

By now, I hope you're starting to get a sense of what Isaiah's big book is all about: it's about making good choices. These early chapters are like massive warning signs saying, 'Here are the consequences of your actions! This is what will happen if you as a nation, as a government, as God's people, or as an individual, make poor decisions.'

I went to Australia last year and at one point, Michele and I found ourselves standing on a beautiful deserted beach by a sign saying, 'Beware! Crocodiles! Do not step within a metre of the water's edge.' Right next to that sign there was another one saying, 'Beware! Box jellyfish!'

Those jellyfish are one of the most deadly creatures on earth and can kill you with one sting. Just as I'm jovially saying, 'I don't think I'll go for a swim today, Michele,' a guy comes up to me and says, 'I wouldn't stand there, mate!' He points up at the palm tree we're standing underneath. 'If one of those coconuts drops on your head, it'll kill ya!' I look around, and all over the beach there are these huge coconuts. There I was in a seemingly beautiful place with these three deadly warnings facing me. Let me tell you, I moved, fast! In this section of his prophecy, Isaiah brings three warnings of the dire consequences of rebellion. Ahaz the king has made some unwise decisions, going directly against Isaiah's warnings and advice. Now God's judgement was coming. Isaiah brings us three pictures of God's verdict that comes upon the nation.

The river, the stone and the dark

First of all we see the picture of a rising river, a frightening flood of judgement. This is chapter 8 verse 7: 'The Lord is about to bring against them the mighty floodwaters of the Euphrates – the king of Assyria with all his pomp. It will overflow all its channels, run over all its banks.' Now historians think there was a literal flood in Isaiah's time but this also refers to a spiritual darkness that seeped overwhelmingly into every part of the nation.

Next, there is a stumbling stone. Chapter 8 verse 14 says this: 'A stone that will cause men to stumble and a rock that will make them fall and for the people of Jerusalem it will be a trap and a snare.' Here we get the sense that men will fall over, just when they think they're strong and standing tall and making decisions. They will find themselves stumbling flat on their faces.

The third warning sign is a picture of a gathering darkness: 'Then they will look towards the earth and will see only distress and darkness and fearful gloom and they'll be thrust into utter darkness.' (Isaiah 8:22). This is a picture of an inherent darkness which gets deeper and deeper as people plunge themselves into ruin by making choices which go against the will of God.

This is where a nation is headed without a church and a national leadership that stays faithful. To bring this up to date, I probably need to have a little rant. I believe it is not a small thing that our society has recently re-ordered the laws of marriage. It is significant because we should not play around with the Word of God. I'm convinced the Bible makes it abundantly clear that the fundamental building block of a successful, blessed society is for men and women to be in monogamous, committed marriage relationships. We play with that at our peril. We can't just move the goalposts because it seems more 'fitting' in a permissive and tolerant society. We can't just sit back as the church of Jesus, and say it doesn't matter – because it does.

Remember mercy

Judgement like this is not God's heart. His nature is always to remember mercy because juxtaposed with all these warnings, threats of gloom and doom and the dire consequences of rebellion there's is the undercurrent of his unfathomable grace.

As a ministry, we are committed to the people of Haiti. Pretty much all our staff sponsor children in Compassion projects. Following the devastating earthquake in 2009, we assisted with the rebuilding projects and we visit at least once every couple of years to see how the team is doing. In Haiti, despite the way the government have treated the people, despite the child sacrifices and the injustice, despite the terrible way the poor are being downtrodden, there are still so many glimpses of grace that just blow your mind when you experience them. God's mercy is having the last word.

Isaiah is warning us of the Haitis in our world – real geographical areas where real physical suffering and real injustice are taking place. All sinful rebellion has consequences. Real people get hurt when those in authority choose to turn away from God and do just what they please. We have witnessed the abuse, neglect and pain of the nation of Haiti. Trust me, it is horrible. But right in the midst of it there is God at work with his grace and mercy.

Isaiah rises to his theme in chapter 9 as he begins to describe such wonderful things. He says in the face of all this gloom, all this distress: 'The people walking in darkness have seen a great light; on those living in the land of deep darkness a light has dawned. You have enlarged the nation and increased their joy; they rejoice before you.' (Isaiah 9:2) and then he goes on in 6 and 7 to say, 'For to us a child is born, to us a son is given, and the government will be on his shoulders. And he will be called Wonderful Counsellor, Mighty God, Everlasting Father, Prince of Peace. Of the greatness of his government and peace there will be no end. He will reign on David's throne and over his kingdom, establishing and upholding it with justice and righteousness from that time on and for ever. The zeal of the Lord Almighty will accomplish this.'

There is a place where there is no more judgement, there is just joy. There is a place where justice and righteousness, hope and life reign forever. I'm going! Are you going? It's a place that God has saved for his chosen ones, his beloved. It's going to be amazing. It's going to be the rule and authority of Jesus as it is meant to be, a place where the greatness of his government will know no end. There will be a day when all things are made right, when it will all make sense. But there is a challenge for us now to see more of that in this life, too. To see the breakthrough of that Kingdom coming – not just as a prayer we say by rote – 'Your kingdom come on earth as it is in heaven,' – but a cry for it! A heart-felt yearning and craving for God to intervene.

I've started so I'll finish

It says in Isaiah 9:7, 'The zeal of the Lord Almighty will accomplish this.' God's going to do it, he's passionate about it, he's zealous about it. But God's also passionate, and zealous that we experience more of this today. He wants us to speak a better word than all the rubbish printed in the press, and to paint a better picture than those who win art prizes and to document a better story than other film-makers. He wants to remind us that even in the midst of neglect, pain and darkness, nothing can separate us from his love. Evil is thwarted and overcome by the great Kingdom of our God every single day as, across the world his light replaces darkness and his hope replaces despair.

The Lord is looking for some people who will share his passion on this, his zeal for the broken, hurting ones to spend all eternity with him. But, more than this, his heart is that we see more of heaven touching earth. We have to remember that when we make our choices, when we cast our votes or pray at our prayer meetings, this is what is at stake.

REFLECTION

1. Do you sense today that God might be warning you about some of your attitudes and behaviour – that perhaps he is challenging you to think more about the consequences of those choices? What do you want to do about that?

2. What do you feel about the changes being made in our society to legalise drugs, make same-sex marriages lawful and other things contrary to the Word of God? What does it make you want to pray? What does it make you want to do? Have you done that yet?

3. The Bible describes God as being slow to anger and abounding in love. Would you say you share those attributes? How would you describe yourself? Are you quick to take offence and do you bear grudges for some time? Perhaps today is the day when you need to confront some past hurt and ask God to help you forgive those who have wronged you.

1. Maybe my attitude to the high needs people, & my attitude to prayer.

2. I think same-sex marriages are wrong. Quite frankly, to me, it's not marriage. I makes me want to pray for a nation based on Christian principles.

3. I find it hard to love Brian & Mary.

PRAYER

Father,
thank you that your nature is so merciful
and that you are fast to forgive me
and slow to be angry with me.
Help me to be an agent for change
in my community, standing up
for those with no voice and helping those
who are treated poorly.
Teach me how to pray and see
your kingdom coming on earth,
as it is in heaven.
Thank you that your Holy Spirit
is my enabler and my friend
as I travel through life, that I am never alone.
I look forward to the day
when I shall see Jesus in heaven,
the prince of peace ruling and reigning
for eternity, but I want others
to experience that too.
Help me take as many people
with me as possible.

Amen

STORY: Open Doors – a World Wide Message Tribe?

The story of what God has been doing over the last few years with The Message is one of 'open doors'. It started with Eden taking root in new places all across the UK. But increasingly we've found that the power really comes when you have the explosive mix of community transformation, creative arts and Christ-centred enterprise, as we've discovered here in Manchester.

In 2013, we launched Message Midlands with young kingdom entrepreneur Seth Pinnock. He's heading up a groundswell of exciting new ministry which will soon include our first Midlands-based Eden and a travelling creative arts team mentored by Jahaziel Elliot. In 2014 we launch Message Scotland at the CLAN Games, organised to coincide with the Commonwealth Games in Glasgow.

And 2014 also saw our first international Message hub up and running. Message South Africa is, we believe, only the first of many future international hubs. In each case, it's obvious that God is accelerating our progress – what took us over twenty years to pioneer here in Manchester is coming together much faster in new places, as God gives us favour.

We long to see generations of urban heroes raised up from Manchester to Cape Town, from Birmingham to Glasgow and beyond, becoming catalysts for gospel transformation wherever they live. Slowly but surely, maybe we really are becoming a World Wide Message Tribe.

EDEN GOES NATIONAL

When God started speaking to us about 'giving away' Eden – in other words, entrusting the vision to more partners to see its impact spreading beyond Manchester – we began exploring partnerships elsewhere across the North of England. So, just over a decade after our first Eden in Benchill, Wythenshawe, we launched Eden Arbourthorne and Eden Buttershaw in Yorkshire, setting a template for the future: an urban neighbourhood in the bottom few percent of the indices of multiple deprivation, a great partner church and funding in place to support a full-time worker for the first couple of years. Lauren, whose story starts on page 84, was one of the first young people Eden Arbourthorne reached and Eden Buttershaw's passionate team leaders Gav and Maz share some of their story starting on page 170.

Today, seven regional hubs are busy about the task of planting new teams, recruiting workers and bringing new life into the nation's hardest-to-reach communities. In London, Manchester, Merseyside, Midlands, the North East, Scotland and Yorkshire and the Humber, we're now seeking that mix of pounds, people and prayer that makes Eden possible. If you want to be really inspired about all that God has done through Eden over the last 15 years or so, get hold of a copy of Matt Wilson's book, *Concrete Faith*.

Launching Eden in the capital presented us with a whole new challenge – another 'p' to add to pounds, people and prayer: 'property'. Having a vibrant missional community in the heart of any neighbourhood requires bricks and mortar, but up until this point, we'd rarely found problems getting hold of suitable housing for our teams. But London is a very different story. Even in the neediest, least desirable neighbourhoods in London, property is oversubscribed and overpriced. When Eden Tollington team leader Jahaziel Elliot moved into a fourth floor, one-bedroom flat near Finsbury Park, he was hit with a bill of over £3000 in deposit, upfront rent and fees. But London's needs are also some of the greatest in the whole country. How were we going to made Eden work there?

It has required a whole new approach, and a whole new level of partnership. One exciting way this has expressed itself is in the London Missional Housing Bond, pioneered by Eden London director Dan Haigh. London is one of the wealthiest cities on earth, with churches often sitting on capital reserves and many wealthy Christians who might be persuaded to invest in missional housing if only they could see the potential. So Dan began work on a new strategic approach to releasing property for urban mission, in partnership with other agencies. The first four hundred thousand pounds has already been raised for urban housing, and, now the system is in place, the team hopes to unlock much more financial resource for mission across the city.

Eden is also playing its part in fulfilling the Diocese of London's Capital Vision 2020, specifically in the area of creating 100 new worshipping communities across London. Though the challenges remain constant, the team are seeing God at work as they seek him and wait for his timing. Enquiries to join teams are picking up, and churches are becoming more open to the possibilities of working together and sacrificing to see breakthrough in the toughest estates.

The first few years of Eden's work in London has been about laying sustainable foundations and getting a few strong teams in place. In spring 2014, we celebrated our first-ever London Urban Hero Awards, with worthy winners coming from across the city and some impressive guests joining us on the night, including cabinet minister Iain Duncan Smith. It really feels like right now we are creating momentum and sowing seeds for what's to come. Relationships are building, partnerships are developing, friendships are emerging, and there's an exciting sense that God's people are genuinely working together towards something amazing in the capital. We know that Eden is just one part of a huge network of kingdom activity across the capital, but we are eager to play our part.

MESSAGE SOUTH AFRICA

In March 2014, we launched our first international hub, Message South Africa. Beginning with prisons ministry around Cape Town and an Eden team in the Salt River neighbourhood, the team has a vision to expand its reach across South Africa as God opens the doors. At the helm is a visionary leader, Tim Tucker, who is building a team of gifted evangelists for Cape Town, but who has an expansive vision for ministry across

South Africa and into the wider African continent. One month earlier, 200 guests had celebrated the launch of the first Message Trust international office in Cape Town, South Africa. I'd gone over to attend the launch and take part in a week of activities and all I can say is 'wow'. It was a week that changed the level of expectation for what God is going to do through The Message there, to the point where, following the launch, Tim and the Message SA team needed to revise all their goals upwards to keep up with all the opportunities. Over the next three years Tim and his team are now trusting God for a massive vision.

Firstly, for an expanding Eden movement into many tough neighbourhoods across Cape Town and into other South African cities. The first Eden team is already being formed and preparing to move into Salt River, an historic neighbourhood just outside Cape Town's city bowl. 80 people attended their first Exploring Eden, and conversations with a number of churches have already taken place that will see new Eden teams recruited and deployed during 2015.

Secondly, for a high-impact prison ministry that will work with juvenile offenders in their pre-release period. This will include clearly presenting the gospel, ongoing discipleship,

and delivering various programmes preparing them for release. Additionally our prison aftercare coordination is partnering with many churches who will supply mentorship and support to offenders once they are released. The programme is being developed in Drakenstein Prison and will seek to provide the hope in Christ to break the cycle of gangsterism, unemployment and reoffending. Also, they have been able to facilitate the launching of a Prison Ministry Alliance which is an umbrella for a number of prison ministries seeking to work together in closer cooperation. This exciting development will greatly increase our impact as we partner with like-minded Christian ministries for greater impact.

Thirdly, a vision for employing the unemployable through Christ-centred Enterprise. Having formed a think-tank of 15 business people, the team are now developing plans to launch a Leadership & Enterprise Centre in 2015. They are now seeking a suitable building that will also serve as the hub of all Message SA activity and plan to be initiating their first business enterprises and apprentice scheme in the coming months. Included in this process are eight former prisoners who are serving as their first 'Oaks of Righteousness' mentorship group (the Oaks) who have all put a life of gangsterism and crime behind them and are seeking to become positive role models in their communities.

Finally, the team will be launching their first Creative Team to provide the missional thrust that needs to take place in all our initiatives. The chosen band members will be trained for six months at the Message Academy here in the UK before being sent back to South Africa to work full-time with the Message SA team. They will serve in schools, prisons and churches.

God has provided miraculously for all of this. We have felt a tidal wave of prayer support over the past few months, with many prophetic words and powerful promises from the Bible that are forming the foundation for the Message SA story. The initial Message SA team of three is expanding as local Cape Townians are joining, including former gangster Kwanele Cement who will work part-time in the prison ministry, and Luleka Domo as administration and fundraising manager. They have been overwhelmed by the support of the first partner church, Jubilee Community Church, and many others. The team have also experienced miraculous financial provision, with their initial faith target for 2014 met at our launch dinner. As their vision is rapidly expanding, so is their faith.

MESSAGE SOUTH AFRICA

YOUR
LIFE
MESSAGE

CHAPTER TEN

ISAIAH 9:8-11:16

'But the people have not returned to him who struck them,
     nor have they sought the Lord Almighty…
for all this, his anger is not turned away,
     his hand is still upraised.'

Isaiah 9:13, 17

'A remnant will return, a remnant of Jacob
will return to the mighty God.'

Isaiah 10:21-22

'The earth will be filled with the knowledge
of the Lord as the waters cover the sea.'

Isaiah 11:9

Hitting the nail on the head

I saiah is now coming back to reinforce what he's already said so far. The skill of a good communicator is to find multiple ways of saying the same thing, over and over again. Why? Well, because we learn by repetition. It's a bit like banging a nail into a wall: the nail doesn't penetrate the surface with one hit; you have to bang the truth in until it's firmly fastened into people's hearts and minds. After a while it can become a bit wobbly again, so you need to hit it back in again and check it has landed well before putting anything weighty on it.

For any of us who have been around a while, especially if we've got a preaching or a teaching ministry, we need to be clear what our 'life messages' are. I have always believed my own to be very simple: 'Keep prayer hot' and 'Keep mission hot'. Whenever I stand up on a platform to speak, the chances are that what comes out of my mouth will have something to do with one, or both, of these themes. As a movement too, we have a life message – and it's lifting high the cross and presenting the beautiful truth of the gospel. We're about constantly finding new and dynamic ways to keep faithful to the incredible message of Jesus.

Reading this section of his book, Isaiah's 'life message' seems to be four-fold…

There is a decision

The first passion of Isaiah is that God's people know that there is a moment of decision. Not long ago, my family and I were in South Africa, and both my kids, Sam and Beth, signed up to do the world's largest bridge bungee jump. It's a very, very large drop – 216 metres, down into a breathtaking canyon. Michele and I, like the wimps that we are, just sat and watched!

Just as Beth was getting ready to do the jump, the girl in line before her completely bottled out. Having paid £80 to get up there, she just decided she couldn't go through with it. All the staff were coaxing her saying, 'Come on, it will be amazing! You will love it!' But she was overcome with emotion. It took another 10 minutes of coaching this girl back to the edge before she finally jumped. Beth, on the other hand, couldn't go quickly enough. It didn't matter that she'd never done a bungee jump in her life, or that this was the world's largest bridge bungee. She just said, 'Arrgh! Let me at it!' And I thought, 'That's my girl!' As they pulled her up afterwards she said, 'That was the best thing I've ever done in my life!'

It's a helpful picture for so many Christians. The moment of decision should be the way Beth did it. We should want to jump in with all we have into the unknown for Jesus, giving it everything we've got; turning away from destructive lifestyles and knowing he is with us. Similarly, I believe there's a moment of decision for the church: we've got to decide that we are jumping! We've got to decide to impact our communities and to make a mark for Christ. There were consequences for refusing God's will 3,000 years ago; and there are consequences today.

There is a judgement

Scarily enough Isaiah's second life message – and you can't get away from it – is that there is judgement for those who reject him. We don't like talking about judgement in these days of grace, but it's all there in the Bible.

Isaiah is strongly concerned with the leaders of the people. It's a fearful thing being a Christian leader. If you're leading any kind of work for God, watch out! We, above all people, need to guard ourselves. When, rather than go God's way, we jump into bed with people like the Assyrians; yoking ourselves with outsiders rather than going God's way with his people, our leadership is going to get corrupted. There will be consequences.

Listen to this in Isaiah 9:14 – 'So the Lord will cut off from Israel both head and tail, both palm branch and reed in a single day; the elders and dignitaries are the head, the prophets who teach lies are the tail. Those who guide this people mislead them, and those who are guided are led astray.'

I think we can see it happening before our eyes. For me there is a real connection between the leadership of some of the authority figures in this nation and the moral decay we see around us. I can't help but think that we must, to some degree, be living under the judgement of God. It's desperately, desperately sad. Why would you want people already struggling in inner-city poverty to be experiencing the judgement that comes from that kind of immoral leadership, oppression and moral decay as well? We are the people who are meant to be taking a lead, helping people through and out of this battle. But to our shame, many of us don't even know we are part of the problem, let alone part of God's solution. We need to wake up and then rise up!

There is a remnant

Thankfully, Isaiah's tone starts to shift at chapter 10, verse 20. After a chapter-and-a-bit of all this judgement and woe come these beautiful verses: 'In that day the remnant of Israel, the survivors of the House of Jacob will no longer rely on him who struck them down but will truly rely on the Lord, the holy one of Israel. A remnant will return, a remnant of Jacob will return to the mighty God.' (10:21-22)

According to Isaiah, there will always be a number of passionate, God-honouring, Jesus-followers who are committed to making good choices every day, even when it's not easy. In Isaiah's day there was only 7,000 of the remnant – they had been decimated.

I don't know about you but I'm excited about the remnant in the UK. We've had generations of decline, but the remnant is ready to be set on fire. This is not the same landscape as when we embarked upon The Message 25 years ago.

You can look around at some of the things that are going on in prisons and in people's lives and estates. You can look at some of the values and some of the stuff in the media and the filth on the Internet and think, 'Oh, woe is me! This is awful!' But there is a remnant! In his name, we are a powerful people that are ready to turn the tide. The Lord wants to say to us, 'Lift your eyes. Look at what I'm doing around this nation. Look at the remnant!'

We are not playing games here at The Message. People's eternal destinies are at stake. The future of a nation is at stake. So we will refuse to sideline the word of God. We will do all we can to put Jesus first. There's a remnant and we want to be part of it. What about you?

There is a heaven

Finally there is a wonderfully poetic and symbolic picture in Isaiah chapter 11 of the future that lies ahead for the remnant people of God. Listen to these amazing words: 'The wolf will live with the lamb, the leopard will lie down with the goat, the calf and the lion and the yearling together; and a little child will lead them. The cow will feed with the bear, their young will lie down together, and the lion will eat straw like the ox. The infant will play near the cobra's den, and the young child will put its hand into the viper's nest. They will neither harm nor destroy on all my holy mountain, for the earth will be filled with the knowledge of the Lord as the waters cover the sea.' (11:6-9)

What a picture of our future! What a glorious inheritance we will have! Don't you want to be there? Well you can, because it is our future, yours and mine if you know Jesus. It's our destiny because of him.

Here's how Isaiah describes him in Chapter 11:2 – 'The Spirit of the Lord will rest on him - the Spirit of wisdom and of understanding, the Spirit of counsel and of power, the Spirit of knowledge and of the fear of the Lord. And he will delight in the fear of the Lord. He will not judge by what he sees with his eyes or decide by what he hears with his ears, but with righteousness he will judge the needy. With justice he will give decisions for the poor of the earth.'

What a beautiful future lies ahead of us!

REFLECTION

1. Do you have a life message or a set of verses that you live by? What are they? How do you feel your life is measuring up to that message at the moment?

2 How good are you at making decisions for Jesus? Do you take your time to obey him, or like Beth, are you able to jump headfirst into what he asks of you? Perhaps think of a time when you were slower to make a stand for him and pray about why. What could you do to speed up your reaction time?

3. How does it make you feel to know that you are part of a remnant of God's people who have the power to change the world? What does it make you want to do and why?

My Life Message

2. I had a hole in my soul. I tried to fill it with drink, then drugs, then money & materialism, even with a perfect family, & then gliding......

......but nothing worked.

I got ambushed by God, & everything changed. Jesus fully-filled my life & now all I want to do is to see other people find the same love & joy & hope as I have.

3. I want to see Southcote & Reading transformed by the love of Christ.

PRAYER

Lord,
thank you that you have given me
a purpose and a life message
that you call me to live out day by day.
I pray that in the areas I now name,
you would help me be more effective
in that calling…
(list some of the things you feel
you need to give to God now.)
Teach me how to live with the knowledge
that I have been given the best inheritance
that can never be taken away from me.
Help me to live in a way that enables others
to reach their potential in you, too.

Amen

'God opened doors for
my future and taught me
to be patient so I could
reach my destination'

The Message South Africa's Operations Director Mark Slessenger shares about Abongile, a young man who is in The Message Trust ex-offender mentorship group in Cape Town.

Abongile is from Philippi, a small community just on the outskirts of Cape Town. It's a community that faces many challenges such as poverty, unemployment, crime and gangsterism. Many young people in Cape Town become disillusioned with life and this has led to high levels of crime and many young people going to prison.

Abongile grew up in a poor family and without a father; this led him to look for affirmation and identity in the wrong places. He, like many other young people in the impoverished areas of Cape Town, got involved in drugs, drinking and eventually crime.

Abongile said that this lifestyle began to take his life on a downward spiral: 'I became so addicted by drugs and alcohol that they controlled my life every day, and housebreaking and robbery became my way of getting money. I was high on drugs constantly and it led to me dropping out of school and I was disconnected from my family.'

This led Abongile to prison, where he joined one of the prison gangs. In the Western Cape many young men in prison are caught up in the 'Numbers' gangs. They operate through three dangerous gangs called the '26s' (money), the '27s' (blood) and the '28s' (sex). It's heart-breaking to see so many young men caught up in these gangs, looking for acceptance and identity in all the wrong places.

Abongile was a '26'-gang member and throughout his time in prison Abongile heard about what Jesus had done on the cross and that he could be forgiven, no matter what crime he had committed. One day Abongile made a commitment to follow Christ in his cell.

The transformation was immediate but did not come without its challenges. 'Coming to faith gave me the boldness to quit the gang and smoking in prison, the gang wanted to stab me but the Lord kept me through the rest of my time in prison.' Abongile began spending time reading God's Word and grew stronger and stronger in his faith, sharing that finding Jesus had an enormous impact on his life. 'My mindset, my heart and my future has changed ever since I met the Lord,' he says. 'Jesus is my Saviour; he is everything to me, He has restored my life mentally and emotionally.' He began witnessing to young men in prison and sharing his love for Jesus with others. It was a joy to see what God was doing in his life.

So often when working in the prisons, young men face enormous challenges once their sentences come to an end. This was no different for Abongile when he was released in March 2010. Without a father figure in his life and coming from a poor family in one of the local communities, the odds were stacked against him.

'Being released brought me many challenges; I was looked at as a disgrace by the community because of what I had done previously. Even my own brother said to me one day that he was scared of me – this was difficult for me to hear.'

"Life before prison"

Life before prison it was about happiness interms of wet worldly standard, living a life of being a party animal. To be drunk and to be under the influence of drugs was my everyday lifestyle. I become so addictive in a point of being controlled by drugs and alcohol, robbery and house breaking become a my way of getting money. being high everyday my life that lead me to be addictive to drugs. That lead me astray cause interupt with my studies. I found myself disconnected with my family cause most of its time i spent with my friends.

Being in prison was the fruit on of my lifestyle, i found myself in the gangsterism cause that is the lifestyle in prison. after being sentenced i came into senses to change the way of living but i didn't know hows, i was not bold to stand for my choice. The life of being a gang member looked nice but the end of that life was rebellion

Accepting the lord at the age of an years restore my life mentaly and emotionaly, I became so bold to quit gang and smoking even though they wanted to stab me, cause they say there is only one way to get in, there is no way out. The lord kept me tough time before bars up until i was released in prison.

Being released living with my family was a bit challenging cause they looked at me with a disgraceful eye even my community was like that It happened one day my brother confessed to me that he was afraid of me when i released earlier but now he is so enjoying to live his life with his big brother. recconecting my family is something that i missed so much, they are behind me, with the process of being build by the lord. The life i live now to work out my life working out my salvation with fear and trembling, trusting in the lord that he is who begin his work in me shall accomplish.

ABONGILE'S STORY

ABONGILE WITH MARK

Although the circumstances at the time were very difficult, he had a strong desire to continue in his education. But how would he be able to afford it?

Thankfully, God opened the door for a bursary with the College of Cape Town and I was able to find funding through a personal friend's family, which allowed Abongile to carry on his studies in electrical training. This was an amazing opportunity for him and he persevered through all the levels of training to complete his it. This meant that he could seek further bursaries to complete the other levels of the course, which he did, of his own accord. Abongile found that it was not easy but learned that God was with him throughout this time: 'God opened doors for my future and taught me to be patient so I could reach my destination,' he says. The dedication he showed to pursue his studies was an inspiration to many of his friends and peers.

In mid-2013, Abongile finished his studies and passed his exams – a wonderful achievement. His mum worked hard to support him during more than two years of study. At the end of it all, Abongile secured a job working for Medi-Clinic and is now working there full time. He has come a long way since prison and continues to dream and trust God for the future. He says: 'The Lord opened the door for me to be an electrician and I would love to open my own electrical and air conditioning company in the future.'

Abongile is a part of The Message South Africa ex-prison mentorship group called 'The Oaks', based on Isaiah 61 verse 3: 'They will be called oaks of righteousness, a planting of the Lord to display his splendour'. On a recent Message camp Abongile shared that he has a strong desire for God to use him in helping other young men out of prison: 'My vision is to have my own business and employ people from my community and guys coming out from prison. I have learnt many skills and believe I have the ability to open my own business, teaching others and helping them learn the skills I have learnt over the past couple of years. I would also like to go into prison and teach the guys skills in electrical, refrigeration and welding and then employ them when they come out.'

This is an amazing vision and fits very closely with the vision of The Message Trust South Africa in supporting young people in and out of prison holistically.

Abongile's life is a testimony to the awesome life-changing power of Jesus and evidence that a life lived in obedience to Christ will always bear tremendous fruit. He is now an active member of his church and often witnesses to his friends and to the men back in Drakenstein, and is volunteering with The Message Trust prisons team. His smile and his joy is all the proof you need that Jesus is the centre of his life.

Seeing what God has done in Abongile's life fills us all with hope and expectation that Jesus will change the lives of many others in prison. There are thousands of men and women in South Africa's prisons who need to know that there is a Saviour who died for them so they can be forgiven and live a new life full of new hope and new meaning.

Pray for Abongile and the other young men and women in contact with The Message's prison ministry in Cape Town.

THERE'S POWER IN PRAISE

CHAPTER ELEVEN

ISAIAH 12:1-6

In that day you will say:

'I will praise you, Lord.
    Although you were angry with me,
your anger has turned away
    and you have comforted me.
Surely God is my salvation;
    I will trust and not be afraid.
The Lord, the Lord, is my strength and my song;
    he has become my salvation.'
With joy you will draw water
    from the wells of salvation.

In that day you will say:

'Give thanks to the Lord, call on his name;
    make known among the nations what he has done,
    and proclaim that his name is exalted.
Sing to the Lord, for he has done glorious things;
    let this be known to all the world.
Shout aloud and sing for joy, people of Zion,
    for great is the Holy One of Israel among you.'

Isaiah 12:1-6

Wired to worship

What if I were to tell you I knew the secret of a successful, joyful existence? Wouldn't you want to know it? Well, I do know! The answer is to choose to be a person of praise.

In the Bible, the Lord himself encourages us to spend a lot of time worshipping. The book is full of exhortations to sing praise to him. What is that all about? Is God on some kind of ego trip or something? Why would He want so much praise? Why does he have seven billion people on this planet, and want every one of them praising him?

I'll tell you why: because it is what we are made for; and it is what makes sense of life. We are wired to be worshippers it is simply the way we are made. The way we will succeed in life, the way we will enjoy life, and the way we will be fulfilled in life, is when we choose to get our eyes off ourselves and focus on our awesome, wonderful, powerful and holy God.

Try chasing anything else and you will never truly be satisfied. But try cultivating a life of praise where through it all, in amongst any amount of garbage that comes your way, you focus your attention on praising and worshipping God – then suddenly life is different, because there is such power in praise.

Twin tracks

Isaiah 12 has two songs of praise within its six short verses: one is an individual song and the other is a corporate one. Interestingly, both songs start with a certain phrase: 'In that day...'. Our praise is based on certain days. It's based on a day in the past, when Jesus came – the Messiah when the promises of Isaiah were fulfilled. It's based on another day in the past when Jesus rose from the dead, and it's based on a future day when the full measure of those promises will be experienced.

Verse 1 and 2 say, 'I will praise you, Lord. Although you were angry with me, your anger has turned away and you have comforted me. Surely God is my salvation; I will trust and not be afraid. The Lord, the Lord, is my strength and my song; he has become my salvation.'

I'd love The Message to be carried forward on twin tracks of strength and song. The first track is strong acts of faith, because God is in us and God is for us. The Lord is our strength, so we're able to do things and push through barriers we could never do on our own. But he's not just our strength; he's our song, too. That's the second track: that everything we do is done with a heart of gratitude. We're always looking for the next opportunity to praise him for who he is.

The truth is, we need both. Ministries that are only about strong acts of faith get a little bit angry and they burn people out. It all gets too much like hard work when it's all strength, and no song. Ministries that are all about song become a bit airy-fairy, they grow increasingly inward-looking, and they never change the world. So, I want to be both. I want us to go in strength, because our strong God is with us, but with a song, carried forward with joy in our hearts.

Salvation's song

If you let me push this analogy just a bit further, as well as two tracks we have a truck. What is the name of this truck? I'll give you a clue. 'He has become my salvation' (v.2) 'With joy you will draw from the wells of salvation' (v.3) What kind of truck is it? It's a salvation truck.

We're a salvation movement. It's actually the only thing we've got that makes us different. Anybody can do prisons work. Anybody can go and live on a tough estate. Anybody can go into schools and teach kids. What's different about us? It's not clever strategies and nice facilities. It's our hope and heart for salvation.

At our Vision Night last year, we got to hear from Mo Timbo. He was one of our first Urban Heroes, a man who found Jesus in prison through our Reflex team and was radically transformed. He'd been a gangster and a drug dealer but after coming out, he got a job, worked hard and joined a good church.

God's hand was on his life. He got married to his girlfriend who he'd been living with and started to bring up his child in the Lord. Before long, his church spotted his leadership potential, and he began to grow a house group in his home. Now he's preparing to plant a church. When salvation breaks out, everything can change!

And this is what it comes down to: we're a salvation people, and if we lose that, we lose everything. As a ministry, and as the body of Christ we must constantly draw with joy from the wells of salvation.

The heavenly business

Now here's the second song: 'In that day you will say, give thanks to the Lord, call on his name. Make known amongst the nations what he's done and proclaim that his name is exalted. Sing to the Lord for he has done glorious things. Let this be known to all the world. Sing aloud and sing for joy people of Zion, for great is the holy one of Israel among you.'

The day we're in is a good day. We're saved, accepted, filled. Jesus is alive. That's enough to make us want to praise. But even the most raving, charismatic, kingdom-chasing, devil-busting Christian knows that 99.9% of our promises are still to come. As we are caught between this day and the day to come, surely we've got to embark upon that heavenly business of praise, because heaven is going to be a place of glory and worship. So we'd better get used to it!

What can touch somebody with that perspective? What can you do to somebody if they've got that vision of Jesus? Nothing! If God is for me, who can be against me? Jesus died on the cross for me! He's alive in me! He's proved himself faithful for all these years! Have you got that vision of Jesus? It's why in the New Testament men and women who truly had that perspective were constantly bursting out in loud praise. They lived on the tiptoes of expectation that any day the kingdom could come and just break in.

He is among you

We need to exhort one another. 'Give thanks to the Lord and call on his name' (v.4) Come on, let's sing our hearts out! Look at our Lord. He's amazing! We need to encourage one another corporately, day in and day out, to give praise to our wonderful God and get involved in this heavenly activity.

We praise him for who he is, and what he does, for his great and mighty acts. But we also praise him for where he is. Here's the final verse of chapter 12: 'Shout aloud and sing for joy people of Zion, for great is the holy one of Israel. He is among you.' He's here with us. The Lord is here, especially present when we join together to sing praise to him and gather around his Word. He's here. I'm a temple of the Holy Spirit and so are you. He's here! The Lord is here. He is here with you right now as you are reading this! We praise him because he's amongst us. If he's amongst us, if he's in us and with us, you know what has to well up within us? Praise!

REFLECTION

1. Do you really know the Lord's strong hand on your life? Is there some area where you're overcoming because of the strength of the Lord? Is there some circumstance in your life of addiction, pain, neglect, frustration, or lack of finance that you are beating, because of his strength in you?

2. Have you also ever experienced the joy of the Lord regardless of your circumstances? Have you ever tried praising God in spite of how you feel rather than waiting until you feel like praising? What was the result?

3. Are you good at reminding others to be grateful, praising people? How could you encourage those around you to praise God this week?

1. Yes, the church is growing, people are coming to faith, people are getting healed, the gospel is being preached.

2. Yes, on the side of the road when the car broke down.
    As a result we got to share our faith with not one, but two people.

3. Get them to remember a time when they've known God's blessing on their lives.

PRAYER

Dear God,
Through every circumstance
of life no matter how hard,
help me to cultivate a life of praise.
Thank you for who you are,
what you do,
and where you are right now.

Amen

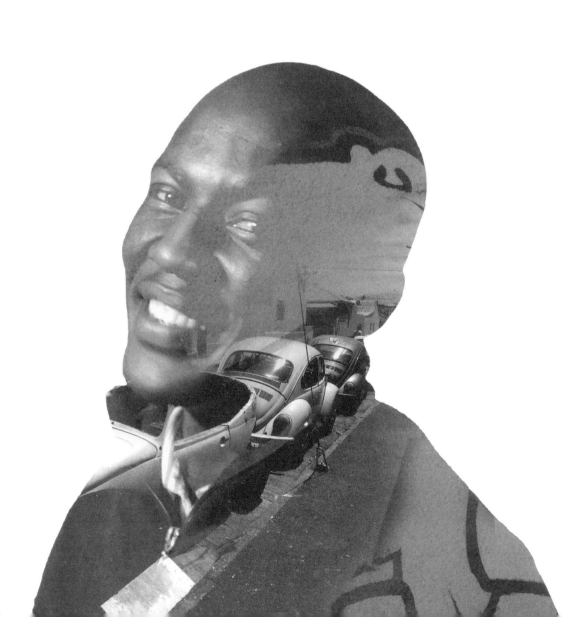

TESTIMONY
GAV & MAZ HUMPHRIES

'God is amazing and he keeps on showing his goodness to us.'

Gav and Maz have been leading Eden Buttershaw in Bradford since late 2009. In that time they've seen God do some amazing things in one of the UK's most deprived communities.

I definitely have a 'Here I am, send me!' story. My life had been one long downward spiral until I finally hit rock bottom and cried out to God for help. When I did, he answered my prayer, and not only healed me and changed me, he set me straight on a path to helping others.

My family life growing up wasn't great – I didn't see much of my dad and he never showed much interest in me. So I began getting into trouble. It started with occasional cannabis use but it wasn't long before I was deep into the drugs world, selling drugs around Glossop to support my habit. At 16, I was kicked out of my parents' home and went from dingy flat to friends' floors to living on the streets.

I wasn't someone you could trust any more. I had a bad reputation and no one wanted to know me. But deep down all I wanted was a relationship with people who cared about me. I got to the point where I was owing thousands of pounds to people, living in a shed, unable to eat or sleep because the drugs had made me paranoid.

Without quite knowing why, I started to yell at God. I didn't even really believe in God, but I didn't know what else to do. I gave him both barrels for three and a half hours – I just told him what I thought of him. By the end I was exhausted. I remember praying, 'If you are who you say you are, get me out of this mess!' And he did – through a random meeting with a lady who looked after me as a kid, I was put in touch with a family who offered me a place to stay – and lots of love.

At one point, a group from Canada came to stay who seemed to have something I needed. I didn't know what it was, but I knew I wanted it. They went off to Maidstone in Kent, and I just followed them. While I was there, I gave my life to Christ. Things just clicked. As soon as I said, 'Right God, I'm willing to give this a go,' my whole demeanour changed. My addiction to drugs was instantly removed. I was totally transformed.

Soon after, God started speaking to me about working with young people, leading to Bible training and opportunities to work in schools and the community. When I first heard about Eden, I knew it was what God had been preparing me for. So in late 2009, my wife Maz and I moved to join Eden Buttershaw, a Bradford estate in the bottom two per cent of deprived wards in England.

It's because of my history that I can relate to kids living here in Buttershaw, one of the most deprived estates in the country. There are a lot of kids growing up without a dad here. Crime and drug use are way above average, and people's lives tend to be chaotic.

Having said that, in the four years we've been here, we've seen some amazing transformation.

We've built on a strong foundation laid by years of faithful investment by Buttershaw

Baptist Church, and in partnership with our local youth centre we're reaching hundreds of young people every week through regular mentoring, discipleship groups, youth bands, free running, youth club, lesson support and an after-school seeker group in the local high school. Two of our young people have won Urban Hero Awards, and in 2013, Maz and I won one ourselves!

But the place where we see the change most clearly in the lives of individuals and families who have given their lives to Christ, got baptised and started bringing change to other people's lives. When we first arrived, the local high school invited us in to help run their CU. There, we met an amazing young girl called Emma who became a Christian through one of our team. She joined in our youth activities at church and Maz started mentoring her. We knew instantly she was a special girl with a deep love for Jesus and a passion to share her faith.

As a result in the change in Emma, before long Emma's mum and stepdad were both believers too, asking to be baptised and to renew their wedding vows because they wanted a fresh start as a family. They instantly 'got' Eden and did the very countercultural thing of moving back onto the Buttershaw estate, having left some years before. They're now a key part of our team, natural evangelists who are faithfully doing the 'little and often' work of loving and discipling young people.

Emma has gone from strength to strength and is now leading her CU. It's in no small part thanks to her prayers and passion that we were recently invited into the school to run a missions week in conjunction with Vital Signs from The Message. The school couldn't praise us enough for the week we put on, impacting hundreds of students, staff, even the governors – it was fantastic. Best of all, at the end of the week gig, 84 kids made a response to the gospel. God is amazing and he keeps on showing his goodness to us.

It's amazing how one family's obedience to the call of God can have a ripple effect on a community like ours. Living on Buttershaw might seem to other people like a sacrifice and, yes, it has its challenges. But Maz and I wouldn't be anywhere else. Having Simeon, our little boy, recently opened up even more opportunities within the community. Births and deaths are the two things that really bring the community together in Buttershaw and we suddenly had people we hardly knew knocking on our door and becoming part of our lives.

God is up to some very exciting things in the urban communities of the UK and we feel very privileged to have a front-row seat. All it's about is making yourself available and willing to say 'here I am, send me.'

GOD'S
GOT BIG
SLEEVES

CHAPTER TWELVE

The Lord will have compassion on Jacob;

once again he will choose Israel

and will settle them in their own land.

Isaiah 14:1

The final couple of chapters of Isaiah we will look at in this book remind me a little bit of an afternoon of Ashes cricket I watched recently. I was really looking forward to the time off and a rare chance to sit in front of the telly for a few hours and watch the match. Sadly, I managed to choose the one day in the whole series that was like watching paint dry, as England tried to close Australia out and force a draw. It was so incredibly boring! Apart from, just every now and again, there would be one blistering ball that would suddenly turn or swing in the air and knock one of the Aussies out. Or a great English batsman would come and smack the ball to the boundary. Suddenly there would be a small shaft of light that got me out of my seat and made me think, 'Okay, I will watch a few more overs of this turgid, miserable match!'

The next section of Isaiah is a bit like that. A little bit dreary and depressing, but punctuated with incredible shafts of light. And I'm forced to remember: five days of cricket is nothing compared to the reality of Isaiah's world. What he's writing about is years and years of a nation's life and serious prophetic words into the people of Israel and her surrounding nations.

Chapters 13 and 14 list prophecy after prophecy against the Babylonians. All the way back to the tower of Babel the Babylonians have been symbolic of every nation, empire, movement or religion that stood against God. There are a lot of them around today, and there were a lot of them 3,000 years ago, too. So we hear God's word to these nations, who were built on arrogance, evil, injustice and lack of mercy. We learn what their eventual outcome will be. In fact, a lot of the 52 verses in these two chapters, show the Babylonians for who they were: 'You think you're so smart. You think you're so clever. You wait till you see what God's going to do with you. You choose this path of arrogance and pride and evil – you just watch what your final outcome will be.'

A shaft of light

Of course, we've read the final page of the Bible. We know where creation is heading. It is moving towards that great and glorious day when God will bring his purposes together in triumphant conclusion! Yet in between, there can be a lot of confusing episodes. There can be gloom and judgement. There can be nations and systems rising up that are blatantly evil, and people living with the consequences of their God-less actions. The Babylonians are the archetypal picture of exactly that – of the kind of satanic arrogance that God always opposes.

Then in the middle of all these terrible prophesies of destruction and torment, announcing the final end of the Babylonians and the nations around Israel that defy God, there is a beautiful little nugget of hope. In the middle of the long, dull afternoon of Ashes cricket, the ball hits the sweet spot, and it's sent out hurling over the stand, and smashes a window somewhere in the car park! It is a beautiful moment. Suddenly in the midst of 52 verses of woe, we get this, verse 14: 'The Lord will have compassion on Jacob; once again he will choose Israel.'

Where did that come from? We've had these terrible woes and judgements and all these disasters that are going to befall God's enemies. Then there's suddenly this little moment: the Lord will have compassion on us. That word 'compassion' in the original language speaks of the highly-charged intimate love of a mother for her child. Is there any kind of love on earth stronger than that?

The Lord will – not *might*, but *will* – have compassion on us because we are his chosen people, his own. But we have to make a choice. We have to decide that in the midst of all that kind of arrogance and pride and evil, a tidal wave going one way – we will go the opposite way. We must continue to choose the way of righteousness and humility. We must work hard to put God first. Here, slap-bang in the middle of all this judgement on the nations heading for destruction, is a group of opposite-spirit people, a chosen people, a people upon whom the Lord has compassion, a people fighting their way towards glory. Are you amongst them?

Living in the opposite spirit

The greatest challenge to the Israelites was, whatever you do, do not make a pact with these surrounding enemies, those evil, arrogant opposers of God. Whatever you do, be set apart. Whatever you do, avoid alliances with those who do not honour God.

At The Message, we love it when people want to give us money to advance our work. But if they want us to be somehow compromised and 'less Christian,' we won't touch it. If there's any hint that there are strings attached to the money that would mean we had to water down our message, we're not interested. We can't have pacts that mean we'll lose our power. We've got to be bold. We've got to stand out. So I'll go to the next meeting and I'll do the same presentation. Yes, I want to do it with winsomeness. Yes, I want to draw people and woo them to the gospel. But we've got to live in a counter-cultural, opposite spirit that affects everything we do, or else we'll never do what we're meant to do.

This affects us at an individual level, too. If we want to be people of humility and righteousness, it will affect the way we treat our wives or our husbands. How can we be miserable and complaining towards our spouses if we're captivated with being righteous, loving, set apart people? It affects the way we operate in every relationship, both at work and at home. How can we be lazy at work if we are truly captivated by him? We're working for Jesus! It affects our thought life. We make every thought captive to Christ. When evil, wicked ideas come in, which of course they will, we take them hostage and we focus on Jesus.

It means we will live differently, knowing that we're chosen and that the Lord takes great delight in blessing his people, and allowing them to stand out. We will choose the path of righteousness and humility. We will be the lamp on the stand that shines in the darkness.

Big sleeves

I mentioned my brother in the introduction to this book because he's been a key part of The Message since day one. He and his wife Julia have been on real journey the last few years (I'm not telling you any secrets here, it's all in his own book, *In The Furnace of Fire*). They've been spending themselves on behalf of some of the most marginalised people in the world, the Dalits of India. They've set up enterprises and a charity that means that many hundreds of the poorest kids in the world are getting an education and a real chance in life. But things haven't been easy for them personally. Over the space of six years, Simon has gone from being a millionaire to losing it all. The credit crunch hit. Everything went pear-shaped. The bank foreclosed on his house and he was going to be forced to sell it for a fraction of what it was worth.

But the same day he reluctantly agreed the much reduced price for his house, a wealthy Christian guy came along and offered him full asking price. In fact, not only that, but he sugested that Simon and Julia could go on living in the house for a peppercorn rent for the next five years, until he moved up from down South to retire there. So Simon and Julia lived in this house for less than you'd pay for the smallest one-bedroom flat in Manchester. It was the favour of God, no doubt about it.

When the time finally came for them to move, God gave them another miracle house. The landlord went so far over the top to bless them it was beautiful. He built an office at the side of Simon's house for the Dalit candles business to run out of. He put a new kitchen in for them and even went so far as to buy them an Aga! I walked round this house with him. It's just amazing. Our mum was there, just crying with joy because this couple who had lost everything had found out that God was strong on their behalf.

I said to Julia, 'I bet you didn't think God had this up His sleeve for you, did you, Julia?' And she replied, 'What I've learnt over the last five years is, God has got very, very big sleeves!'

I love that, don't you? God's got very, very big sleeves for his chosen people. If we will pursue righteousness and keep going with his strength and a song in our heart; if we'll choose to do it with humility, he'll bless us.

How can we give him maximum glory? If we try and grab the Lord's glory for ourselves, we're never going to be blessed the way we should. But if we will try our best to keep him central, keep his gospel central, lift high the name of Jesus, give him all the glory, all the credit, then God's got some amazing stuff up his sleeves for us.

Isn't it great to be part of God's family; to be working it out as we proclaim the gospel; working it out as we love the poor and serve the most marginalised and the needy?

REFLECTION

1. How did God choose you? Can you think back over your own testimony and thank God again today for your journey? What were you like before Jesus and what, or who are you like now?

2. Can you think of a time recently when you had to operate in the opposite spirit to something going on around you? What did you learn through that experience?

3. How does it make you feel to learn that God has 'big sleeves' for you? How have you seen him bless you in the past? Praise Him today for his unchanging faithfulness to you!

NOTES

PRAYER

Lord,
as an individual standing before you today,
I want to thank you for reminding me of my own story.
Thank you for choosing to choose me!
Thank you for picking me up out of the gutter
of my own past and putting me
into a wonderful present and a glorious future.
God I am so excited about the big,
big sleeves of your mercy, your grace
and the promises of your Word over me.
Teach me how to be that lamp on the stand
that refuses to be extinguished
and help me burn brightly for you
for the rest of my days.

Amen

The Message Trust

The Message Trust is a worldwide movement with a passion to share Jesus Christ with the hardest-to-reach young people. Through a dynamic combination of creative mission, community transformation and Christ-centred enterprise, we witness to the transforming power of the gospel of Jesus in words and actions.

The mark of a life changed by Jesus is the desire to see others changed too. Time and time again, we see young people going from being the problem to the solution thanks to our work. Many members of our mission teams were once drug abusers, dealers or violent criminals themselves.

We celebrate our stories in print through Flow magazine and in books like this one; online at www.message.org.uk and through regular podcasts; and at special events such as our annual Urban Hero Awards in Manchester and London.

What began as a single schools team in Manchester in the early 1990s has multiplied over the last two decades to include:

Cutting-edge creative missions teams, using music, dance and theatre to community the Christian message relevantly

Dozens of incarnational Eden teams, moving teams of youth workers into tough neighbourhoods in urban areas

A pioneering Enterprise Centre, offering training, employment and discipleship to young people in need of a second chance

During 2013, we announced new Message hubs in the English Midlands and in Scotland, and in March 2014 we launched our first international hub in South Africa.

Will you
help to write
the next chapter?

Want to see more of what you've been reading about?

Want to look back and say, 'I was a part of that'?

Let's make some history together.

COME

Join our Message Academy and discover your part in God's mission.
Ten months of intense training and frontline mission placements in the dynamic,
faith-filled atmosphere of The Message in Manchester.

www.message.org.uk/academy

GO

Called to urban neighbourhoods? Eden needs you.
Join the UK's gutsiest mission movement and bring the hope of the gospel
to forgotten communities. Join an existing team or lead a new one.

www.eden-network.org

GIVE

Become a regular supporter and stand with us long term.
Hear the big news first through our regular Flow magazine,
and receive priority invitations to our annual Vision Night and supporter events.

www.message.org.uk/give

PRAY

Prayer is the fuel to all we do.
Sign up to receive our bi-monthly Prayer Calendar.

www.message.org.uk/pray

For more information on all the above, you can also call 0161 946 2300